Research Report

Developing Army Leaders

Lessons for Teaching Critical Thinking in Distributed, Resident, and Mixed-Delivery Venues

Susan G. Straus, Michael G. Shanley, James C. Crowley, Douglas Yeung, Sarah H. Bana, Kristin J. Leuschner

Prepared for the United States Army
Approved for public release; distribution unlimited

T0308349

RAND ARROYO CENTER

The research described in this report was sponsored by the United States Army under Contract No. W74V8H-06-C-0001.

Library of Congress Cataloging-in-Publication Data is available for this publication.

ISBN 978-0-8330-8152-0

The RAND Corporation is a nonprofit institution that helps improve policy and decisionmaking through research and analysis. RAND's publications do not necessarily reflect the opinions of its research clients and sponsors.

Support RAND—make a tax-deductible charitable contribution at www.rand.org/giving/contribute.html

RAND® is a registered trademark.

RAND OFFICES
SANTA MONICA, CA • WASHINGTON, DC
PITTSBURGH, PA • NEW ORLEANS, LA • JACKSON, MS • BOSTON, MA
DOHA, QA • CAMBRIDGE, UK • BRUSSELS, BE
www.rand.org

Preface

The Command and General Staff Officer Course (CGSOC) is a key component of the U.S. Army's system for developing critical knowledge, skills, and abilities in its officer corps. However, attendance at resident courses is generally not possible for Reserve Component officers. Thus, the Command and Staff General School offers non-resident alternatives for the Common Core: an advanced distributed learning (ADL) course delivered online and a course combining in-person instruction and distributed learning taught in The Army School System (TASS).

This report describes a set of studies designed to evaluate the CGSOC Common Core and to compare educational outcomes in resident, TASS, and ADL delivery venues. The report will be of interest to those involved in planning, developing, delivering, and evaluating leader education and for other courses that emphasize instruction of critical thinking skills.

This research was sponsored by the U.S. Army Training and Doctrine Command and was conducted within RAND Arroyo Center's Manpower and Training Program. RAND Arroyo Center, part of the RAND Corporation, is a federally funded research and development center sponsored by the United States Army.

The Project Unique Identification Code (PUIC) for the project that produced this document is HQD115813. Correspondence regarding this report should be addressed to Susan Straus (Susan_Straus@rand.org).

For more information on RAND Arroyo Center, contact the Director of Operations (telephone 310-393-0411, extension 6419; FAX 310-451-6952; email Marcy_Agmon@rand.org); or visit Arroyo's website at http://www.rand.org/ard.html.

Contents

Appendixes

Figures

Tables

Executive Summary

The Command and General Staff School (CGSS) within the Command and General Staff College provides the Command and General Staff Officer Course (CGSOC) (formerly called Intermediate Level Education), which is a key component of the U.S. Army's system for developing these and other critical knowledge, skills, and abilities in its officer corps. The Common Core, which is the first phase of CGSOC, is taught in three venues: a resident course taught at Fort Leavenworth and at satellite campuses; The Army School System (TASS), primarily for Reserve Component officers, taught by the U.S. Army Reserve Command's 97th Brigade and its three subordinate battalions; and Advanced Distributed Learning (ADL), a web-based, self-paced course that uses interactive multimedia instruction. CGSOC consists of nine blocks of instruction taught as stand-alone modules in the resident course and organized into three phases in TASS and ADL.

In response to the interests of Army leadership, this study sought to answer the following questions about the Common Core, focusing on the 2009-2010 academic year:

- Based on current methods of evaluation, how effective is the Common Core, and to what extent are there differences among delivery venues?
- Based on current measures, how can course delivery be improved?
- How well do current methods of evaluation gauge course success and point to needed improvements?

To answer these questions, we analyzed available data from CGSS, including responses to student surveys, grades on assignments, and student characteristics. In addition, we conducted a quasi-experimental study to assess consistency in grading among faculty members.

Students in All Venues Were Generally Satisfied with the Common Core

Students in all venues generally reported that the course contributed to their learning. Students were also satisfied with other aspects of the course, including the quality of exams and other assignments and instructional delivery. While there were some statistically significant differences among venues, these differences were small and are not practically significant.

However, there were a few differences in students' responses across venues. Students in ADL had lower ratings of the extent to which they felt that feedback enhanced their learning. In addition, some TASS and ADL students reported technical and administrative problems with the interactive multimedia instruction (IMI) portions of the course. Responses to open-ended questions revealed differences not captured in objective questions; for example, dissatisfaction of TASS students with the workload during Phase II of the course (which meets for one weekend per month for eight months) and the desire for peer interaction among ADL students.

Student Grades Were High Across all Venues; Reliability Across Graders Needs Improvement

Analysis of grades on assignments showed that average grades were generally high (ranging from 88 to 92 out of 100). There were no meaningful differences in grades across venues. Whereas grades can, in principle, reflect objective measures of learning, information about students' levels of knowledge and skills at the outset of the course or use of a control group is needed to draw conclusions about how the course contributes to student learning. The average scores on assignments also suggest that there is grade inflation. Thus, assessments may not reflect whether students mastered the course content, and these "ceiling effects" limit the ability to discriminate among levels of performance or to observe associations with other variables.

Moreover, meaningful comparisons of performance require that faculty use the same standards and grading practices within and among venues. We conducted an exploratory, quasi-experimental study examining the consistency of grading among faculty on four assignments. Although the number of faculty who participated in the study was quite small, responses of those who did participate showed that reliability across these graders was generally quite low.

Future Evaluation Should Focus on Whether the Best Possible Outcomes Within Venues, Rather Than Equivalent Outcomes Across Venues, Are Achieved

We found few meaningful differences in students' self-assessed learning and course grades among the three venues. However, these results should not be interpreted to mean that the venues are equally effective or that differences do not exist. Several factors make it difficult to draw firm conclusions about venue differences, including fundamental differences or confounds among venues in factors that may influence learning and attitudes (e.g., use of different learning approaches, different types of students in each venue), potential biases in surveys responses (e.g., leniency in ratings, careless responding, and survey fatigue – which likely are due to the number and length of surveys administered in the course), and low inter-rater reliability in grades.

Moreover, we would not expect the venues to have equivalent outcomes. Although the learning goals are the same, the venues are designed to support different student environments and needs. Given inherent confounds and the demanding data requirements to allow a robust comparison of venues, coupled with the expectation that the Army will have an ongoing need to provide the Common Core in different venues, we recommend that future evaluations focus on whether the best possible outcomes within venues, rather than equivalent outcomes across venues, are achieved.

Suggestions for Improvement Address Course Design and Supports As Well As Course Evaluation

Some results point to strategies to improve the Common Core. First, CGSS should continue recent efforts to examine grading practices and, if needed, provide professional development to ensure that faculty grade to a common standard. Second, CGSS should investigate the use of blended learning strategies, such as those used in their Advanced Operations Course, to provide ADL students with opportunities for instructor and peer interaction. Third, CGSS should address technical issues with access to and functions of online courseware; moving the learning management system from a dotmil to a dotcom domain, as CGSS is doing, can improve speed and reliability. The demands of Phase II on TASS students also warrant further investigation, along with consideration of mitigation strategies such as changes in course structure.

Evaluation can also be improved. Specifically, surveys used in the Common Core can be modified to obtain more diagnostic information:

- Assess self-efficacy questions before and after training in combination with individual-level explanatory variables to assess knowledge gain.
- Reduce response burden in surveys by asking fewer detailed questions and by sampling students to complete the surveys.
- Move from five- to six-point response options for close-ended questions to increase variability in responses.
- Analyze responses to open-ended questions to better understand students' experiences in the course and to improve future surveys.
- Use web analytics, such as response time per question, to assess the quality of responses.

Finally, CGSS can conduct more comprehensive evaluations. Most important is consistently collecting information on the effect of training on job performance by conducting surveys of graduates and supervisors to evaluate whether graduates' knowledge or performance changed after the course. Study findings also indicate the need for better infrastructure for monitoring and evaluation within CGSS to obtain consistent or reliable data through better integration among data sources, use of standardized measures within and across venues, and sufficient staff with knowledge and skills in survey development and analysis.

Extended Summary

The complexity of the full-spectrum operating environment means the U.S. Army's education system must increasingly foster adaptability and critical thinking skills. The Command and General Staff School (CGSS) within the Command and General Staff College (CGSC) provides the Command and General Staff College Officer Course (CGSOC) (formerly called Intermediate Level Education or ILE), which is a key component of the Army's system for developing these and other critical knowledge, skills, and abilities in its officer corps. Completion of CGSOC is required for promotion to lieutenant colonel. CGSOC is made up of two distinct phases: the Common Core course and a branch or functional specialty qualification course, based on the officer's career path. The Common Core, which is the focus of this report, has learning objectives that encompass a broad range of the complex skills and knowledge areas needed to prepare officers to serve on operational-level staffs. The objectives are taught across six instructional themes or blocks: Foundations; Strategic Environment; Joint, Interagency, Intergovernmental And Multinational (JIIM) Capabilities; Doctrine; Joint Functions and Planning; and three cross-cutting or parallel instructional blocks: History, Leadership, and Force Management.

The Common Core is taught in three venues: resident, The Army School System (TASS), and Advanced Distributed Learning (ADL)

- **Resident Courses.** These courses are taught at Fort Leavenworth over 16 weeks and at satellite campuses at Forts Belvoir and Lee in Virginia, Fort Gordon in Georgia, and Redstone Arsenal in Alabama over 14 weeks. Each course block is taught as a stand-alone unit of instruction.
- **TASS.** Reserve Component (RC) officers from the Army National Guard (ARNG) and U.S. Army Reserve (USAR) as well as Active Duty officers (by exception) have the option of completing the Common Core by attending a three-phase course taught by the U.S. Army Reserve (USAR) Command's 97th Brigade and its three subordinate battalions. The course blocks are organized into phases; Phases I and III are taught in two-week Active Duty for Training (ADT) sessions; Phase II relies on eight weekend sessions in an inactive duty training (IDT) or ADT status or on discretionary time in addition to ADL independent study lessons completed on discretionary time. The course takes place over 12 to 18 months.
- **ADL.** Managed by CGSS's Directorate of Distance Education (DDE), the ADL course uses asynchronous, interactive multimedia instruction (IMI). The course is completely web-based. Like TASS, the blocks are organized into three phases. The course is self-paced, takes up to 18 months to complete, and is completed on discretionary time for most students. Except for grading of written assessments and a help desk, there is no interaction among instructors and students.

Army leadership was interested in better understanding the relative effectiveness of these different venues and the Common Core course as a whole. This study compares outcomes of three Common Core delivery venues, examining both the quality of the course as well as the quality of the measures used to assess it. This study sought to answer the following questions about the 2009-2010 academic year Common Core:

- Based on current methods of evaluation, how effective is the Common Core, and to what extent are there differences among delivery venues?
- Based on current measures, how can course delivery be improved?
- How well do current methods of evaluation gauge course success and point to needed improvements?
- How can evaluation be improved to support course goals?

To answer these questions, we conducted analyses based on available data, including analysis of responses to surveys administered to students in resident, TASS, and ADL venues; examination of grades on assignments within and among venues; and the association of student characteristics and performance. In addition, we conducted a quasi-experimental study to assess consistency in grading among faculty members.

Characteristics of the Common Core Venues

The three venues - resident, TASS, and ADL - all have the same learning goals, objectives, and instructional blocks as well as the same readings and scenario materials. In contrast, the venues vary in a number of factors in addition to delivery media and student characteristics. Understanding how the venues differ is important for interpreting results of our analysis of student outcome data.

We found differences across the Common Core venues in a number of areas, including instructional approach, types of assessments used, and course schedules and length. Table S.1 summarizes the key differences across venues.

The most significant differences are between ADL and the other venues. Compared to the ADL venue, resident instruction has students with more years of military experience, more opportunities for collaborative learning and discussion, fewer constraints on student time, and more opportunities for facilitation by instructors with substantial resources at their disposal. Resident instruction and TASS both use the Experiential Learning Model (ELM; Kolb, 1984), which is a collaborative learning approach. In contrast, the ADL course uses an independent learning approach, with no student-instructor or student-student collaboration; self-paced IMI replaces instructor presentations and class discussions of reading materials. Students in the TASS venue tend to have lower levels of operational experience than do resident students as well as more competing demands on their time (especially in Phase II); TASS also has fewer developmental opportunities for instructors. Another significant difference concerns the timing of the course. Resident students complete the course over a contiguous 16-week period, whereas, for both TASS and ADL students, the course is spread over 12-18 months. ADL students, and to a lesser extent TASS students, must also complete significant portions of the coursework on discretionary time.

Table S.1. Summary of Differences Across the Three Venues

	Resident	TASS	ADL
Instructional approach	ELM-collaborative learning	ELM-collaborative learning	IMI-individual learning
Assessments	Individual and group	Individual and group	Individual
Course scheduling and length	Contiguous and completed in about 4 months Coursework can generally be completed in close to an 8-hour day	Three phases over 12-18 months Phases I and III two-week ADT; Phase II 8 weekends plus ADL lessons (self-paced) Longer and more consecutive days during Phases I and III (compared to resident)	Three phases over 12-18 months Self-paced For most students, completed on discretionary time
Instructors and instructor development	Full-time, 60/40 civilian/ military specialists Extensive formal and informal development	Part-time, Reserve generalists in non-deployable status Full formal and limited informal development	Adjunct, generalists (not instructors) used to grade assessments Limited formal and informal development
Instructional support	Online course materials for instructors and students Excellent facilities and equipment support	Online course materials for instructors and students Generally equivalent facilities and equipment for Phase I and III; varied for Phase II	Online materials for students No facilities Full-time help desk

These differences are significant enough that they would logically lead to expectations that learning outcomes and student reactions and attitudes about the course will differ among venues. This prediction is supported by other research that asked graduates from the different venues to compare their experiences in the Common Core with the follow-on course they took in a single venue – distributed blended learning – which combines IMI with synchronous and asynchronous collaborative activities. Responses suggest that students value opportunities for interaction with instructors and peers in that graduates from ADL had the most favorable reactions toward blended learning, and graduates from the resident course had the least favorable reactions (Straus et al., 2013). However, as discussed below, we did not find the types of differences in learning outcomes and student reactions that we anticipated in the present study.

Student Surveys: Perceived Learning and Satisfaction with Training

The CGSS evaluation process relies heavily on student surveys. The surveys are comprehensive, addressing students' self-assessments of learning from the course, reactions to the quality of instructional delivery, quality of assessments, and other aspects of course delivery, such as experiences with technical aspects of the courseware. We analyzed the surveys administered in each venue, including responses to close-ended (objective) and open-ended questions. These surveys were administered online on an anonymous basis after each block (in resident instruction) or phase (in TASS and ADL).

Students in all venues generally reported that the course contributed to their learning. Students were also satisfied with other aspects of the course, including the quality of assessments (e.g., exams and other assignments), and instructional delivery. Many of the results show statistically significant differences among venues, as denoted by asterisks in Figures S.1 – S.4 below. However, with few exceptions, the effect sizes were small, indicating that differences among venues were not practically significant (i.e., are not meaningful). For example, Figure S.1 shows students' ratings of perceived cognitive learning for a sample of measures. The results for these topics as well as for those taught in other phases indicate that students in all venues felt that the course contributed to their learning, with average ratings of approximately 4 or higher on a 5-point scale.

Figure S.1. Perceived Cognitive Learning in Phase II Across Venues

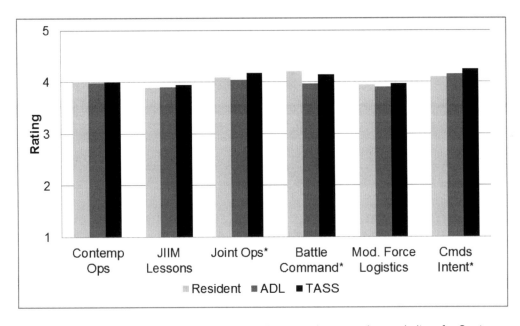

NOTES: Ratings ranged from 1 = strongly disagree to 5 = strongly agree. A sample item for Contemporary Operations" was "I can explain Joint Force Capabilities in contemporary operations."
$*p < 0.05$

Figure S.2 shows students' ratings of the quality of assessments in the course. Students generally reported high levels of satisfaction with exams and assignments.

Figure S.2. Perceived Quality of Assessments Across Venues

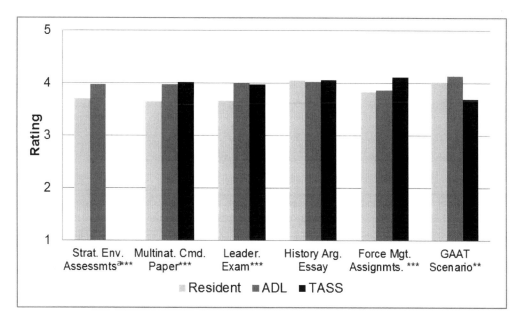

NOTE: GAAT is Georgia-Armenia-Azerbaijan-Turkey.
[a]Responses for TASS Phase I were eliminated because of the low response rate.

$**p < 0.01, ***p < 0.001$

Figure S.3 shows ratings of the quality of instructional delivery. Students gave favorable ratings of instructional delivery in all venues, again, with little practical significance in differences across venues.

Figure S.3. Ratings of Instructional Delivery in Resident, ADL, and TASS Venues

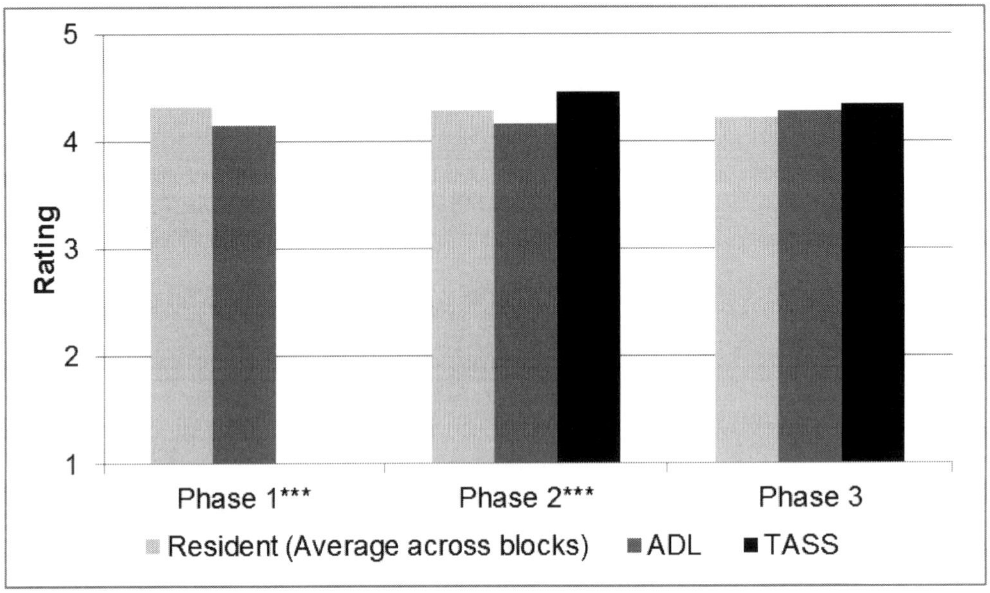

***p < 0.001

However, ratings of the perceived value of course feedback differed by venue. Ratings of the extent to which students felt that feedback enhanced their learning were lower in ADL compared to resident instruction in Phase I (data for TASS were not available) and compared to both resident instruction and TASS in Phase II.

In addition, some TASS and ADL students reported technical and administrative problems with the IMI portions of the course. Figure S.4 shows the percentage of students who reported difficulties with technical and/or administrative aspects of the ADL lessons in ADL Phase I and II and in TASS Phase II. The percentage of students reporting problems was lower in ADL than in TASS, presumably because ADL students have more experience with the courseware. For ADL students, the technical difficulties reported most included problems registering for the course and submitting assignments. In contrast, more than 15 percent of TASS respondents reported difficulties with a number of different technical issues with the courseware.

Figure S.4. Percentage of ADL and TASS Students Reporting Technical and/or Administrative Difficulties

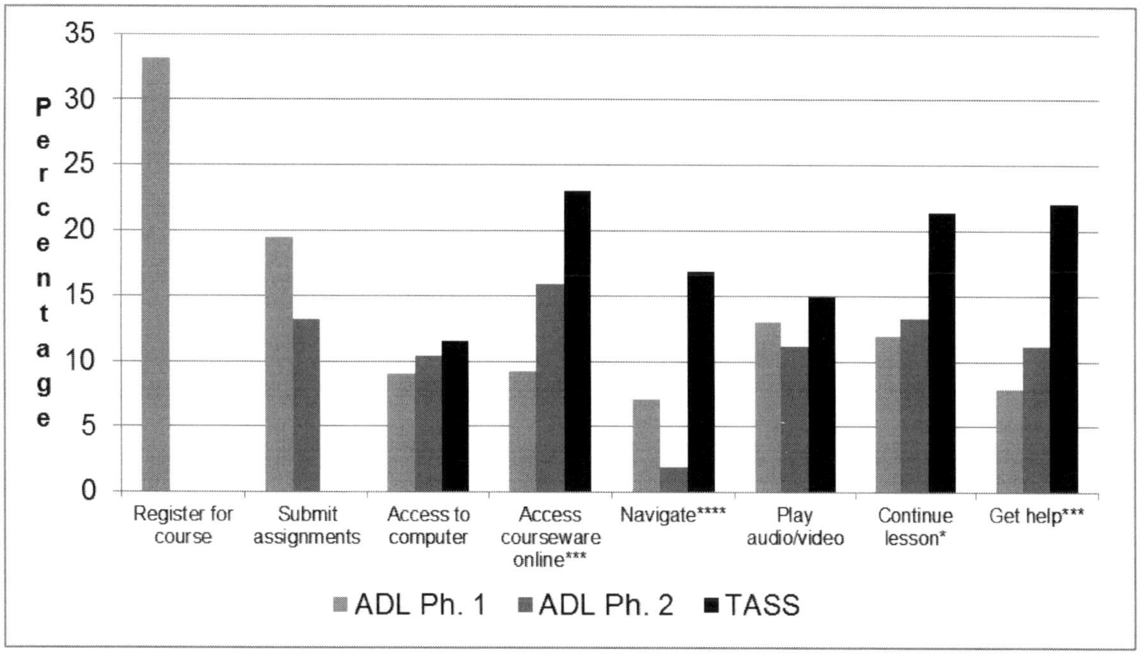

*p < 0.05, ***p < 0.001

Responses to open-ended questions in the ADL and TASS surveys were used to supplement analysis of objective questions. A substantial number of students answered these questions, and many wrote extensive comments. These responses were used to explore the answers to objective questions in more depth, e.g., comments point to sources of students' dissatisfaction with feedback on assessments, such as a lack of timely feedback or uncertainty about graders' expectations. Responses also identified topics or issues that were not captured in objective questions. Two pervasive themes were (1) the amount of work required in Phase II for TASS students, who reported experiencing stress due to role conflict and negative consequences of the workload on educational outcomes; and (2) the desire for (or for TASS students, the value of) peer interaction in the course. Students also offered suggestions for improvement in the course, such as returning graded assignments within two weeks, offering a two-week ADT alternative for TASS Phase II, and providing collaborative tools for ADL students.

Overall, results showing few practically significant differences in survey responses across venues might be used to conclude that the three modes of delivery are equally effective. However, there are a number of factors that make it difficult to draw conclusions about course effectiveness and to interpret the results. First, responses capture students' *perceptions* of learning, but these are not a substitute for *objective measures* of learning (e.g., Sitzmann et al., 2010b).

Second, whereas the survey results could indicate high levels of satisfaction, the responses could also reflect biases such as leniency. Patterns of responses also suggest careless responding (e.g., as shown by strings of the same response across questions) and survey fatigue (e.g., as shown by more missing responses to the second half of the surveys compared to the first half). These patterns likely are due to the number and length of the surveys and the specificity of many of the questions.

Third, conclusions about comparisons of instructional media are ambiguous because of inherent differences in characteristics of students who enrolled in each venue. Students may have also had different expectations for the course depending on the venue in which they were enrolled and adjusted their ratings of the course accordingly. These factors, in combination with systematic differences in course structure and delivery methods described in more detail below, impede making meaningful venue comparisons.

Despite these issues, some measures, particularly in combination with responses to open-ended questions on the surveys, do point to potential areas for improvement in the Common Core. These include providing better and more timely feedback in ADL and TASS, better training and/or support for TASS students on the use of ADL lessons, and continued analysis and consideration of alternative structures for Phase II.

Grades on Student Assessments and Faculty Grading Practices

Accurate and reliable grades are important for several reasons: to motivate students' efforts and to provide feedback about their strengths and needs for improvement, to enable course developers to identify blocks of instruction or lessons for which improvement may be warranted, and to reward outstanding student performance. We analyzed differences among venues in average grades on 11 exams or assignments that were common across venues.

The analysis found that average grades were generally high (ranging from 88 to 92 out of 100) for most assignments in all venues. There were no meaningful differences in grades across venues, and, with the exception of age, there were no systematic associations of grades and individual-level characteristics. Older students tended to earn lower grades on all but two of the assignments assessed. This effect occurred in all venues but was stronger for students in the resident venue than in TASS and ADL.

Significant associations of age and grades, coupled with differences in the distributions of individual-level characteristics across venues, underscore the difficulty in isolating the effects of venue and point to the need to control for differences in the characteristics of students. Furthermore, whereas grades can, in principle, reflect objective measures of learning, information about students' levels of knowledge and skills at the outset of the course or use of a control group is needed to draw conclusions about the effectiveness of the course with respect to learning in all venues.

The average scores on assignments also suggest that there is grade inflation, i.e., that the instructors are lenient in grading. Thus, assessments may not reflect whether students mastered the course content, and these "ceiling effects" limit the ability to discriminate among levels of performance or to observe associations with other variables.

Moreover, there are differences in instructor characteristics across venues that may influence grades. To gauge student performance and conduct meaningful comparisons of performance across venues, faculty must be using the same standards and grading practices within and among venues – goals that are likely to be particularly challenging when assessing intangible skills such as critical thinking. We present results from a quasi-experimental study examining the consistency of grading among faculty on four assignments in the Common Core. We consider the findings exploratory because the study had a low response rate, coupled with the fact that most participants were resident instructors. **Results showed that reliability across these graders was generally quite low.** For two of the four assessments, there was little or no relationship among scores across faculty members who evaluated the same student assignments. Despite the exploratory nature of the study, the results point to the need for further investigation of grading practices in the three venues.

General Conclusions and Suggestions for Improvement

A central finding from our study is that analysis of students' self-assessed learning and grades on assignments and tests show no meaningful differences in outcomes among the three venues. **Although there is often a tendency to want to compare distributed learning and resident instruction, these results should not be interpreted to mean that the venues are equally effective or that differences do not exist. For the reasons cited above, we cannot draw firm conclusions about levels of learning or about reactions or attitudes among students in the three venues.** To summarize, these reasons include fundamental differences or confounds among venues in factors that may influence learning and attitudes, biases in surveys responses, low inter-rater reliability in grades, and a lack of information about student characteristics. **Moreover, although course designers or administrators may seek to confirm findings of "no differences," we would not expect the venues to have equivalent outcomes.** Although the learning goals are the same in all venues of the Common Core, the venues are designed to support different student environments and needs.

Given that the Army will likely have an ongoing need to provide the Common Core in different venues, we recommend that the focus of future evaluations be on whether the best possible outcomes within venues, rather than equivalent outcomes across venues, are achieved. The data requirements to conduct robust comparisons of venues are very demanding, and given confounding factors among venues, it is likely infeasible to control for all of the important differences. With this premise in mind, we provide suggestions for the Common Core in three areas: improvement in instructional delivery and course structure, improvement of current methods of evaluation, and recommendations for additional methods and metrics for evaluation.

Improving the Common Core

Ensure that faculty are consistent in grading. Although findings from the study of reliability in grading may be considered preliminary, the exceptionally low levels of inter-rater reliability indicate the need to investigate grading practices further and to take steps, such as professional development, to achieve greater consistency among faculty and to ensure that instructors grade to a common standard. CGSS has made some changes to address these issues including increasing the role of full-time faculty in ADL (in grading as well as for student coaching and mentoring) and by sampling graded assignments to be re-graded by a second instructor.

Consider providing ADL students with opportunities for instructor and peer interaction by using distributed blended-learning strategies. There are many ways to provide opportunities for such interaction in an online context, either synchronously or asynchronously. In fact, CGSS has already developed a distributed blended learning course with dedicated instructors for the follow-on course to the Common Core, Advanced Operational Concepts (AOC). AOC uses include online synchronous sessions with the entire class and for small group collaboration as well as threaded online discussions about course topics among students with instructor oversight. CGSS should evaluate the costs (e.g., need for additional resources, especially instructors) and benefits of these approaches for use in the Common Core.

Address technical issues with ADL access and functions. For ADL students, the primary difficulty was registering for the course, which is accomplished via the Army Training Requirements and Resource System (ATRRS). TASS students experienced a number of technical problems with ADL lessons, which suggests the need for a more stable network, training or tutorials on use of the courseware, and greater availability of technical support (or increased awareness of existing resources for technical support). In fact, CGSS is moving the ADL lessons from a dotmil to a dotcom domain, which has improved speed and alleviated technology reliability issues.

Consider alternative structures for Phase II. The length and complexity of Phase II and its impact on ADL and TASS students warrant further investigation, along with an evaluation of mitigation strategies. CGSS has studied these issues and has implemented improvements. Examples of additional changes that might be considered include offering Phase II in an additional ADT session for TASS coupled with fewer IDT sessions and supplementing an all-ADL Phase II option (currently being offered) with some of the blended learning methods discussed above. These alternatives have pros and cons in terms of such factors as cost, student preferences, and burden on students that need to be studied further.

Improving Evaluation of the Common Core

Modifications to the surveys could enhance their usefulness as part of a comprehensive program of evaluation. We propose recommendations to obtain more diagnostic information from surveys and reduce response burden, and we recommend use of additional measures to assess course effectiveness.

For questions about cognitive learning, consider administering self-efficacy questions before and after training in combination with individual-level explanatory variables. Measures of self-efficacy or self-assessments of absolute knowledge (rather than self-assessment of knowledge gain) are more strongly associated with cognitive learning outcomes than are measures of learner reactions (Sitzmann et al., 2008; Sitzmann et al., 2010b). However, measuring self-efficacy only at the end of a course may reflect pre-existing knowledge rather than knowledge gain. A stronger approach is to administer the same questions before and after training along with demographic characteristics and other individual-level explanatory variables associated with academic performance, such as general cognitive ability, learning goal orientation, and motivation to learn (measured at the beginning of the course).[1] These explanatory variables can also be used in analyses of student performance (grades). These measures need to be collected on an identified basis in order to link responses collected before and after training. In other words, we are suggesting that the self-efficacy survey be administered separately from the course/instructor satisfaction survey (discussed below).

Administer a separate, anonymous survey at the end of the course to assess satisfaction with training. This survey would focus on reactions to training (e.g., questions about satisfaction with assessments and instructional delivery) along with a limited number of demographic characteristics and related variables including component, rank, highest degree, age, career field, payment status (i.e., personal or duty time) while taking the course (for ADL and Phase II TASS students), and questions about time available to work on the course (ADL and Phase II TASS). These explanatory variables would need to be included in each survey, as anonymous participation would preclude linking responses across surveys. Separating satisfaction questions to be collected on an unidentified basis will encourage candid responses from students.

For questions about cognitive learning – whether about self-efficacy or perceived knowledge gain – administer fewer detailed questions about each topic or ask more global questions. Asking many specific questions will produce data with limited variability and will likely result in low response rates, cursory responses, or missing data. Given that students appear generally satisfied with the course, it also may not be necessary to ask extremely detailed questions unless feedback is needed regarding a change to the course. Since this study was completed, CGSS has, in fact, reduced the length of the surveys.

Reduce response burden further in the resident course by sampling students to complete each survey in the resident course or by administering different subsets of items to students in ADL and TASS (as CGSS did in Phases II and III). Response rates might be

---

[1] Note that one, pre-training survey should be administered in the resident course rather than administering a survey before each block of instruction.

higher if students are aware that they will be asked to complete fewer or shorter surveys. CGSS has implemented sampling in their survey practices for the resident since this research was completed and reports improved response rates.

For close-ended questions measuring reactions to the course, move from five to six response options, e.g., "strongly disagree," "disagree," "disagree somewhat," "agree somewhat," "agree," and "strongly agree." More options are preferable for Likert-type scales because validity and reliability improve as the number of response options increases, up to seven (Lozano, García-Cueto, and Muñiz, 2008), and an even number of options eliminates the middle, ambiguous response of "neutral." In a recent study of another CGSOC course, we found less leniency bias and more variation using a six-point scale, which can enhance the diagnostic value of responses (Straus et al., 2013).

Analyze responses to open-ended questions to gain a more thorough understanding of students' experiences in the course and to identify issues not addressed in objective questions. CGSC currently performs manual analysis of subjective responses. There are a variety of analytical tools that provide automated ways to mine these types of responses and provide more efficient and systematic analysis.

Add objective questions about topics that emerged from responses to the open-ended questions or to diagnose patterns of responses to objective questions (such as higher perceived difficulty in Phase II for ADL students). For example, it may be useful to include close-ended questions about topics such as students' family and job commitments and time available to work on the Common Core and to examine correlations of these responses with changes in self-efficacy or post-course reactions.

Finally, use web analytics to assess the quality of responses to course surveys. Response time per question or for the survey overall could indicate whether students appear to be devoting sufficient time to completing the survey or whether they seem to be "clicking through" the items. Transition of the learning management system to a dotcom will enable CGSS to assess time spent on the survey.

Other Methods and Metrics for Evaluating the Common Core

Collect follow-up information and evaluations from graduates and other stakeholders. Conducting surveys of Common Core graduates sometime after completing the course (e.g., after 6 or 12 months) can be used to seek their assessment of how the course has affected their jobs. CGSC has conducted surveys of graduates in the past, and we recommend doing so on a more regular basis and undertaking a systematic analysis of results. Likewise, supervisors can be surveyed to evaluate whether they have observed any difference in graduates' knowledge or performance. Examining the association of performance in training with graduates' subsequent judgments or supervisors' ratings could provide a way to assess the impact of training on job performance.

Use web analytics for ADL lessons. Data collected in many learning management systems can be used to assess student behavior in the course (e.g., time on lessons, number of logins) and its association with performance. CGSS could also track student completion rates and time to completion of phases, particularly in ADL where students are responsible for their progress through the course.

The reliability of data for monitoring training outcomes, as well as some of the difficulties we have reported in obtaining consistent or reliable data, indicate the need for better infrastructure for monitoring and evaluation within CGSS. Evaluation could be facilitated through better integration among data sources, use of standardized measures within and across venues, and sufficient staff with knowledge and skills in survey development and analysis.

Concluding Thoughts

Evaluation is an important process in training and education to support improvements in course design and delivery. This study demonstrates many of the challenges in evaluating educational outcomes, particularly for courses that focus on complex cognitive skills. It also demonstrates the difficulties of comparing instructional venues in a field setting in which delivery methods and other factors are inextricably bound. Where these inherent differences exist, future evaluation should focus on whether the best possible outcomes within venues, rather than equivalent outcomes across venues, are achieved.

Acknowledgments

This project would not have been possible without the assistance of many people in the Army distributed learning community. We wish to thank Daniel Ward for his extensive support and contributions to this project. We are also grateful for the expertise, time, and effort from Nellie Goepferich, Rick Steele, COL Thomas Kallman, and many Command and General Staff Officer Course faculty members. This study also benefited from the efforts of other RAND colleagues. We especially wish to thank Brian Stucky and Donna White for their contributions to this project. Finally, we thank Traci Sitzmann and Mike Thirtle for their comprehensive and insightful comments on an earlier version of this report.

Abbreviations

AC	Active Component
ADL	Advanced Distributed Learning
ADT	Active Duty for Training
AER	Academic Efficiency Report
AGR	Army/Guard Reserve
ANOVA	analysis of variance
AOC	Advanced Operational Concepts
ARFORGEN	Army Forces Generation
ARNG	Army National Guard
AT	Annual Training
ATRRS	Army Training Requirements and Resource System
BCS	Battle Command Systems
CAC	Combined Arms Center
CGSC	Command and General Staff College
CGSOC	Command and General Staff Officer Course
CGSS	Command and General Staff School
DA	Department of the Army
DDE	Directorate of Distance Education
DL	distributed learning
DoD	Department of Defense
ELM	Experiential Learning Model
FDP	Faculty Development Phase
GPA	grade point average
ICC	intraclass correlation
IDT	Inactive Duty Training
IMI	interactive multimedia instruction

ILE	Intermediate Level Education
JIIM	joint, interagency, intergovernmental and multinational
JOPES	Joint Operation Planning and Execution System
JOPP	Joint Operation Planning Process
JPME 1	Joint Professional Military Education Level 1
JSPS	Joint Strategic Planning System
MDMP	Military Decision Making Process
ns	not statistically different from zero
MEL 4	Military Education Level 4
PCS	permanent change of station
PME	professional military education
RC	Reserve Component
SD	Standard deviation
SOF	Special Operations Forces
TADLP	The Army Distributed Learning Program
TASS	The Army School System
TLO	Terminal Learning Objective
TRADOC	Training and Doctrine Command
USAR	U.S. Army Reserve
USARC	U.S. Army Reserve Command

1. INTRODUCTION

The complexity of the full-spectrum operating environment means the U.S. Army's education system must increasingly foster adaptability and critical thinking skills. The Command and General Staff School (CGSS) within the Command and General Staff College (CGSC) provides the Command and General Staff Officer Course (CGSOC) (formerly called Intermediate Level Education or ILE), which is a key component of the Army's system for developing these and other critical knowledge, skills, and abilities in its officer corps. CGSOC is the Army's formal Professional Military Education program, which supports the development of junior field grade officers who are adaptive leaders, capable of critical thinking, and prepared to operate in full-spectrum Army, joint, interagency, intergovernmental and multinational environments.[2] Completion of CGSOC is required for promotion to lieutenant colonel. Officers who successfully complete CGSOC have Military Education Level 4 and Joint Professional Military Education Level 1 (JPME 1) designations annotated on their personnel records, and this makes them eligible for assignment to many key joint and Army positions.

CGSOC is made up of two distinct phases:[3] the Common Core course and a branch or functional specialty qualification course, based on the officer's career path. The Common Core prepares the officer for the follow-on qualification course (Advanced Operational Concepts, or AOC). The Common Core is also designed to "move junior majors from a tactical perspective to an operational perspective so they can rejoin the field force as effective field grade officers."[4]

CGSS offers the Common Core as a traditional resident course; however, the Reserve Component (RC) environment generally precludes attendance at centralized resident courses. Thus, CGSS has historically offered alternatives to the resident course, including a blended learning course consisting of resident and online instruction in The Army School System (TASS), and a self-paced, online course, called Advanced Distributed Learning (ADL). Army leadership was interested in better understanding the effectiveness of the Common Core as a whole and the relative effectiveness of the three delivery venues.

Prior RAND research has documented the need for comprehensive and systematic assessments of training effectiveness to determine whether students obtain requisite knowledge and skills; to identify areas for improvement in curriculum content, instructional methods, and processes; and to provide information for attainment of long-term objectives. When implementing alternative approaches to professional military education (PME), documenting

---

[2] See Headquarters, U.S Department of the Army, 2009.

[3] Some students also have to take four short preparatory courses.

[4] The description of the Common Core contained in this chapter is primarily based on Headquarters, U.S. Army Command and General Staff College, 2009.

effectiveness is important to ensure that educational objectives are met, to gain stakeholder buy-in, and to establish the case for appropriate levels of resources. RAND has conducted several recent assessments of distributed learning (DL) effectiveness across a range of Army courses (e.g., Shanley et al., 2012; Straus et al., 2009, 2011). CGSOC is distinct from most of the courses examined in these efforts because it is concerned primarily with development of more abstract critical thinking and problem-solving skills, which are inherently difficult to teach and to assess.

Purpose of This Study

This study supports the Army's program development efforts in leader education by comparing outcomes of three CGSOC Common Core delivery venues: resident instruction, TASS, and ADL. This project examines both the quality of the Common Core as well as the quality of the measures used to assess it. Thus, a central focus of this report is analysis of the methods used to evaluate the Common Core and improving the evaluation process. Findings are relevant to this and other courses with similar learning objectives and to courses that use alternatives to traditional resident instruction.

Research Questions and Overall Approach

This study sought to answer the following questions about the 2009-2010 academic year CGSOC Common Core:

- Based on current methods of evaluation, how effective is the Common Core, and to what extent are there differences among delivery venues?
- Based on current measures, how can course delivery be improved?
- How well do current methods of evaluation gauge course success and point to needed improvements?
- How can evaluation be improved to support course goals?

The sources of data and research tasks used to answer these questions include the following:

- **Analysis of surveys administered to students.** We present results regarding the psychometric properties of the surveys, students' post-training attitudes about the extent to which the course enhanced their learning and their reactions to features of instructional delivery, and differences in these responses across venues.
- **Analysis of levels of performance, in terms of grades on assignments**, as well as the association of student characteristics and performance.
- **Results of a study of grader consistency across delivery venues.** In the Common Core, evaluation of students' critical thinking skills are based largely on essay tests and written exercises, which are inherently subjective to grade (compared to multiple choice tests, for example). There are systematic differences in the characteristics of graders in each venue, and if there are corresponding differences in how graders interpret or apply grading standards, then comparisons of learning outcomes across venues may be ambiguous. This study uses a quasi-experimental design to assess consistency in faculty members' quantitative ratings and qualitative comments on students' assignments.

In the following sections, we describe the learning objectives of the Common Core and provide more information about the three venues (in-depth descriptions of the venues are presented in Chapter 2). We then present the overarching framework and prior empirical findings that guided our evaluation efforts.

CGSOC Common Core: Learning Objectives and Venues

All Common Core venues use the same learning goals, objectives, readings, and scenario materials. Learning objectives are extensive and encompass a broad range of the complex skills and knowledge areas needed to prepare officers to serve on operational level staffs. These skills require student learning at high cognitive levels. In terms of Bloom's (1956; 1994) cognitive levels, knowledge and comprehension levels are required, but most learning objectives entail application, analysis, and even synthesis. The Common Core primary or Terminal Learning Objectives (TLOs) are summarized in Appendix A.[5]

CGSOC Common Core's learning objectives are taught across the course's nine instructional blocks or themes. The focus of each block is described in Table 1.1, along with the approximate number of course hours devoted to each. All three venues have the same blocks, but they are organized somewhat differently; blocks are taught as stand-alone units in the resident course, whereas in TASS and ADL, they are organized into Phases. Phase I consists of Foundations (C100) and Strategic Environment (C200), Phase II consists of Joint, Interagency, Intergovernmental and Multinational (JIIM) Capabilities (C300) and Doctrine (C400), and Phase III consists of Joint Functions (C500) and Planning (C600). History, Leadership, and Force Management blocks are taught mainly in Phase II, but some of these lessons are taught in other phases.

---

[5] The summary of block learning objectives comes from Headquarters, U.S. Army Command and General Staff College, 2009.

Table 1.1. CGSOC Common Core Learning Objectives

Block	Class Hours	Description
C100 Foundations	36	• Makes students aware of contemporary operating environment • Refines reasoning, critical thinking, problem solving skills • Includes lessons on leader development, media relations, operational law, civil-military operations, persuasive writing
C200 Strategic Environment	34	• Addresses learning areas prescribed by service intermediate-level colleges • Introduces joint, multinational, and interagency environment • Discusses concepts for perceiving, understanding, and analyzing strategic military challenges • Contributes to the appreciation of organizations, processes, and products that define the military instruments of national power
C300 JIIM Capabilities	26	• Develops skills for using JIIM capabilities • Examines JIIM limitations and strategic and operational interagency and multinational capabilities and considerations
C400 Doctrine	54	• Examines fundamentals of joint operations with emphasis on operational art and design • Examines fundamental principles of Army operations and impact of enemy forces • Includes lessons on modular force logistics, commander's role in battle command, tactical concepts of full-spectrum operations • Includes application of operational design to the Guadalcanal Campaign
C500 Joint Functions	17	• Focuses on joint functions of command and control, intelligence, fires, movement and maneuver, protection, sustainment, and information operations • Includes application of each of the joint functions in the context of a joint operational scenario
C600 Planning	62	• Focuses on practical application of military decision making using tools of the Joint Operation Planning Process (JOPP) and the Army's Military Decision Making Process (MDMP)
F100 Force Management	18	• Develops officers who are prepared to lead, affect, implement, articulate, and manage Army change • Builds understanding of strategic, operational, and tactical aspects of organizational transformation
H100 History	18	• Covers "Rise of the Western Way of War" • Provides broad perspective on interplay between war and Western society and nature of revolutionary military change • Introduces student to military theory (e.g., Jomini, Clausewitz)
L100 Leadership	26	• Focuses on challenges faced by field grade officers in developing and leading organizations • Addresses how field grade officers can influence the development of organizations

Although course content, readings, and materials are essentially the same across venues, in the early phases of our research, we discovered that each venue uses a different instructional approach, timeline, and environment.

- **Resident Courses.** These courses are taught at Fort Leavenworth over 16 weeks and at satellite campuses at Forts Belvoir and Lee in Virginia, Fort Gordon in Georgia, and Redstone Arsenal in Alabama over 14 weeks. The course at Fort Leavenworth has two start dates per year, while each satellite site has three start dates per year. Approximately 2,500 officers participate per year (1,450 at Fort Leavenworth). Most students at Fort Leavenworth are operational career field officers in the Active Component (AC); students at satellite campuses are typically functional area officers and officers in other career fields.[6] Some RC officers, officers from other services or countries, and civilians also take the resident course.[7]
- **TASS.** Reserve RC officers from the Army National Guard (ARNG) and U.S. Army Reserve (USAR) as well as Active Duty officers (by exception) have the option of completing the Common Core by attending a three-phase course taught by the U.S. Army Reserve Command's (USARC's) 97th Brigade and its three subordinate battalions. The course is taught over 12 to 18 months. Officers can switch off between TASS and ADL (described next) from one phase to another. Approximately 2,500 officers participate per year.
- **ADL.** Managed by CGSS'S Directorate of Distance Education (DDE), the ADL course uses asynchronous, interactive multimedia instruction (IMI). The course is completely web-based. Like TASS, it is taught in three phases; it is self-paced and takes up to 18 months to complete. Except for grading of written assessments and a help desk, there is no interaction among instructors and students. DDE manages course execution through Blackboard, a web-based content management system that delivers the courseware and provides supporting material to instructors and students.[8] Approximately 3,000 officers participate per year.

Theoretical and Empirical Background

Theoretical Background

As a framework for this evaluation, we used a model of training evaluation and effectiveness proposed by Alvarez, Salas, and Garofano (2004) that is applicable to diverse types of training and that we have used in prior research (see Straus et al., 2011, for a detailed description of the

---

[6] Operational career field officers are in branches that are assigned to the operational force, that is, units and organizations directly supporting deployment, employment, and sustainment of land forces. Officers in other career fields and functional areas are trained, developed, and educated to support more specialized assignments in the institutional portion of the Army.

[7] The current operational environment makes it difficult for AC officers to attend resident CGSOC in a timely way, so the ADL option is also being used by AC officers.

[8] Blackboard Inc. is an enterprise software company that develops educational software, in particular learning management systems. CGSS uses a Blackboard system for the Common Core.

model).[9] The model articulates outcome measures to evaluate training and factors that may influence or explain these outcomes. Evaluation is important because it indicates whether a course meets its intended goals. For example, evaluation might show how satisfied students are or whether the skills learned transfer to the job. Measuring explanatory factors, such as student ability, motivation, or alternative methods of instruction can point to reasons for outcomes, e.g., why students are more or less satisfied with a course or why knowledge or skills acquired during the course do or do not affect subsequent job performance. Assessing these reasons enables designers, developers, and instructors to modify aspects of the course such as prerequisites, curriculum, or delivery in order to improve outcomes.

This study of the Common Core focuses on three types of evaluation measures in the Alvarez, Salas, and Garofano (2004) model: *reactions to training*, *post-training attitudes* or self-assessments of learning, and *performance in the course* as reflected by grades on course assignments. These measures target the first two levels in Kirkpatrick's (1994) four-level classification of training outcomes (reactions, learning, behavior or on-the-job performance, and results).

We also examine factors that affect training outcomes. Alvarez, Salas, and Garofano (2004) posit three types of explanatory factors: individual, training, and organizational characteristics. Examples of individual characteristics include abilities, demographics, experience, motivation, and personality traits. Training characteristics refer to factors such as instructional media, instructional style, opportunities for practice, and feedback provided to students. Organizational characteristics include factors such as the climate for learning, training policies, facilities, and administrative procedures (e.g., course registration). In this study, we focus on individual characteristics (demographics and experience) and training characteristics (instructional media).

Prior RAND research on Army DL has evaluated course content and design via use of expert judgments and learner reactions (Straus et al., 2009; 2011), cognitive learning (Straus et al., 2011), and efficiency in terms of course utilization rates and course development cycle time (Shanley et al., 2012). This study extends some of this prior research, which focused largely on skills training, to outcomes in officer education. At the request of Army leadership, a primary focus of this study is on training characteristics in terms of comparing outcomes among resident, ADL, and TASS delivery venues.

Empirical Studies

Venue comparisons. There is some preliminary evidence that addresses differences in venues for leader education from the 2010 Center for Army Leadership annual survey of Army education graduates (Hatfield et al., 2011). Overall, results indicated that respondents had favorable views of CGSOC in general. In comparison to graduates of other Army leadership

---

[9] This model is relevant for training of concrete knowledge and skills as well as education of more abstract concepts or processes.

courses, graduates of CGSOC were more satisfied with several aspects of the courses, such as learning how to influence others, acquiring improved leadership capabilities, and currency of course content than were graduates of other Army leadership courses. In addition, similar percentages of respondents reported that Army institutional education effectively prepared them for higher levels of leadership responsibility, regardless of whether they participated in resident instruction, distributed learning, or blended learning.[10] However, leaders who attended courses in resident venues, either in whole or in part, rated the quality of instruction more favorably than did leaders who participated in the course via DL.

More broadly, there is a large, although inconclusive, research literature on how delivery medium influences the effectiveness of training and education. Several studies have compared instructional media for adult learners (e.g., Phipps and Merisotis, 1999; Straus et al., 2006; Wisher et al., 1999) and have found no clear advantage for resident instruction or DL. However, as these authors have noted, the research literature has suffered from numerous weaknesses, including a lack of objective measures of learning, the use of convenience samples rather than random assignment, small sample sizes, low response rates or differential response rates in venues, and insufficient evidence about the reliability and validity of measures. In addition, findings of no differences between venues cannot be interpreted reliably to mean that resident instruction and DL are equally effective because one cannot confirm the null hypothesis, and many studies comparing venues lack sufficient statistical power to conclude with confidence that a lack of differences between conditions is meaningful.

More recently, researchers have published meta-analyses of studies comparing classroom and online learning for adult learners (Means et al., 2009; Sitzmann et al., 2006). Both of these meta-analyses found that on average, students in online learning conditions performed better than those receiving face-to-face instruction.[11] However, as in other reviews, many of the studies had methodological weaknesses. Although Means et al. (2009) identified more than a thousand empirical studies of online learning published from 1996 - 2008, only 51 studies met their criteria for inclusion in the analysis, which included comparison with a face-to-face condition, objective measurement of learning outcomes (rather than self-report), a rigorous research design, and statistical information needed for meta-analysis. In the Sitzmann et al. (2006) analysis, only a small number of studies were true experiments in which students were randomly assigned to training conditions. Moreover, in the true experiments, the effects of medium were reversed, such that students performed better on tests of declarative knowledge in resident instruction than in DL. Thus, in the quasi-experimental studies in Sitzmann et al. as well as in other reviews, results showing no differences between venues or better performance in DL may have been due to factors such as selection biases, i.e., systematic differences in students who take the course in

---

[10] These responses were from CGSOC and Army War College courses.

[11] In Sitzmann et al. (2006), this finding held for knowledge about declarative knowledge (knowledge about facts) but not for procedural knowledge (knowledge about processes).

each medium. This is an important consideration in Army research, given that there may be factors that influence who enrolls in one venue or another.

Clark and Mayer (2011) argue that the instructional methods, not the delivery medium, are the primary determinants of learning. Learning programs are effective when instructional strategies are designed to be compatible with human learning processes. Thus, they would expect DL and classroom education, for example, to show similar learning outcomes when each approach is designed to support psychological processes of learning (which we anticipate might be accomplished in somewhat different ways). We would add that each approach must use an instructional design that is suitable for the complexity of the material presented.

Explanatory variables. In addition to examining instructional media, where possible we examine associations of individual-level explanatory variables with reactions, attitudes, and performance. There is a large body of research documenting the association of individual characteristics and success in adult education. Examples include general cognitive ability (e.g., Ree, Carretta, and Teachout, 1995; Ree and Earles, 1991); age (Arulampalam, Naylor, and Smith, 2004; Hoskins, Newstead, and Dennis, 1997; Koch, 2006); gender (Arulampalam, Naylor, and Smith, 2004; Cantwell, Archer, and Bourke, 2001; Hoskins, Newstead, and Dennis, 1997); race (Miller and Ewell, 2005; Talbert-Johnson, 2004); learning goal orientation (e.g., Fisher and Ford, 1998; Klein, Noe, and Wang, 2006; Mesmer-Magnus and Viswesvaran, 2007; Phillips and Gully, 1997); motivation to learn (e.g., Klein, Noe, and Wang, 2006; Noe, 1986), and other responsibilities, such as work and family obligations (Fairchild, 2003; Martinez-Caro, 2011; Wilson, 1997). In this study, we were limited to a small number of demographic and experience variables captured by CGSS.

In the chapters that follow, we will discuss specific ways in which we applied the principles described in this section to our analyses of student survey results and differences in grades across venues.

Organization of This Report

The remainder of this report is organized as follows:

- In Chapter 2, we describe the three venues that are the subject of this investigation, highlighting differences that may influence student reactions, post-course attitudes, and performance in the course.
- In Chapter 3, we describe the student survey instruments, analysis approach, and results.
- In Chapter 4, we present results of analyses of student grades in resident, TASS, and ADL venues and the quasi-experimental study of grader consistency.
- In Chapter 5, we summarize our findings, present conclusions, and discuss ways to improve the Common Core and how it is evaluated.

2. OVERVIEW OF DELIVERY VENUES FOR THE COMMAND AND GENERAL STAFF OFFICER COURSE COMMON CORE

In this chapter, we compare features of the three venues – resident, TASS, and ADL – in which the Common Core course is taught.[12] This examination focuses on factors that vary across venues and that logically could have an effect on the level of student learning in the course in general and on student grades and student survey responses in particular. The information presented in this chapter will provide a foundation for discussions in later chapters.

A key point that emerges from this chapter is that there are differences across the Common Core venues in many areas, including instructional approach, types of assessments used, and course schedules and length. These differences are substantial enough that they would logically lead to expectations that learning outcomes and student reactions and attitudes about the course (discussed in Chapters 3 and 4) would differ among venues. We will describe these differences throughout the chapter and discuss their implications further at the end of the report.

The research effort for this comparison included (1) document review, primarily the Common Core syllabus but also briefings and papers provided by the CGSS staff;[13] and (2) an extensive set of informal interviews with CGSS, 197th Brigade, and USARC staff and faculty members. These interviews were performed to expand on the background provided by the document review and to ensure that our comparisons were comprehensive and accurate.

We describe differences in the design of venues across a range of factors that might affect learning outcomes. The factors we examine are:

- Instructional approach
- Assessments of student learning
- Scheduling and time constraints
- Instructors and instructor development
- Instructional support

Instructional Approach

Regardless of venue, course designers strive to use methods that are learner-centered and experiential. Table 2.1 summarizes some of the key features of the learning environment in each venue.

---

[12] In this chapter, we restrict our discussion of "resident" to the Common Core at Fort Leavenworth, as we did not examine instruction at the satellite campuses.

[13] These included Headquarters, U.S. Army Command and General Staff College, 2009, 2005, 2011.

The key difference across venues concerns the level of interaction between students and instructors and among the students themselves. Resident instruction and TASS both use a collaborative learning approach, whereas ADL uses IMI instead of instructor presentations and class discussions of reading materials.

Table 2.1. Features of Instructional Approach and Learning Environment

Venue	Key Features
Resident	• Uses Experiential Learning Model (ELM) • Classroom provides an environment for active learning using the Socratic method • Students are organized into 16 member staff groups with a mix of branches/services for group projects and discussion • Classroom time emphasizes discussion of reading materials, student operational experience
TASS	• Uses ELM and follows same the principles as resident instruction • Formation of staff groups is constrained by geographic location, especially in Phase II • Compared to resident, more diversity in instructor and student experience (i.e., less military experience, but more experience in civilian government and business positions)
ADL	• Uses same reading and scenario materials as other venues • IMI is used in place of instructor presentations and classroom discussions • Completion of automated checks on learning, practical exercises, graded assessments, and tests are used to in place of collaboration and to provide experiential learning activities

Resident and TASS

Resident and TASS instruction are based on the Experiential Learning Model (ELM) (Kolb, 1984). In this model, the classroom is conceived as an active learner environment in which faculty members serve as subject matter experts and facilitators of collaborative learning, and student/faculty discussion is expected to stimulate thought and knowledge construction to achieve the course goals of critical reasoning and creative thinking skills.[14]

Most classroom hours are devoted to instructor-facilitated discussions, student and student group presentations, and practical exercises. Individuals and groups also prepare projects and presentations during and outside of class, which they must explain and defend to the instructor and other staff group members. To manage group projects and discussions, students are organized into staff groups, each of which contains 16 students (two staff groups are joined for exercises and selected instructor-led classes). Staff groups are composed of students with a wide range of experience. Fort Leavenworth classes have sister service and international officers in each staff group.

Both resident and TASS venues benefit from the experience that students bring to the classroom. The resident course consists predominantly of AC officers, the majority of whom are

---

[14] See Headquarters, U.S. Army Command and General Staff College, 2011.

in the operational career field. Resident staff groups typically represent a broad mix of branches and operational experience as well as students from different services, nations, and government agencies. Having a wide range of student experience in staff groups is considered important by CGSS staff because it provides a broad base of collective knowledge that can contribute to all students' learning. Several CGSOC instructors stated that the sharing of group knowledge is often more important than the instructor's contribution for many course themes. Some instructors reported that they frequently learn a great deal from their students, especially regarding recent operational methods.

Because the majority of TASS students are in the RC, many typically have less military experience than do students in the resident venue. On the other hand, RC officers attending the Common Core are more likely to have experience relevant to many important general and some full-spectrum learning goals (e.g., experience in relevant civilian leadership positions, such as government and business). However, the TASS environment puts more constraints on the formation of staff groups with a broad range of experience and backgrounds. In particular, the formation of staff groups is limited by geographical location, especially in Phase II, which is taught at a large number of dispersed locations. Unlike resident CGSOC, the same TASS staff groups cannot be kept together throughout the course, and new groups are formed at the beginning of each phase.

ADL

ADL has the same reading and scenario materials as the resident and TASS courses; however, there is no student-instructor interaction or peer collaboration. Instead, ADL uses automated and ungraded checks on learning and practical exercises to substitute for classroom participation. Checks on learning include multiple-choice questions and drag-and-drop-exercises in which the student matches an answer from a group of responses to a group of categories. Another check on learning involves the student writing a response to a question. In this case, a correct answer is shown and the student can compare the correct response with his or her own.

Whereas collaborative learning approaches are not currently used in ADL, there are some areas in which its IMI instruction can be advantageous. For example, the use of well-developed IMI, such as a video of a talented, recognized subject matter expert, can arguably provide better and more standardized instruction than can be provided by a wide range of staff group instructors. Indeed, CGSS staff is considering using some of the IMI presentations in resident instruction. In addition, an individual working alone in IMI is required to complete all of the work, whereas students working collaboratively may free ride on the efforts of others.

Assessments of Student Learning

Graded student assessments in resident and TASS differ from those in ADL. The primary difference is that assessments in resident and TASS venues consist of both individual and group assignments, whereas ADL relies exclusively on individual work. Grading is also done by different types of CGSOC staff across venues. In both TASS and resident courses, course instructors grade assignments, whereas in ADL, assessments are either graded by computer or by part-time adjunct faculty. Table 2.2 highlights the different types of assessments used, which are discussed in more detail below. Differences in faculty characteristics are discussed in more detail in the section on instructors and instructor development.

Table 2.2. Types of Assessments Used in Resident/TASS Compared to ADL Venues

Resident and TASS	ADL
Class participation	None
Group presentations and briefings	None
Individual presentations and briefings	None
Individual multiple choice test	• Many more • Automated tests on subject areas
Individual written assignments	• Same as resident plus additional assignments • Students assigned a portion of resident group assignments and complete them individually

Resident and TASS

As indicated in the table, resident and TASS courses use the same five types of graded assessments. Except for class participation and group efforts, all of the graded written assignments are done outside of classroom hours and are open book. There is one multiple-choice test, and the rest of the individual graded assignments consist of written essays, planning documents, or short-answer responses.

The balance of assessments varies by block of instruction and lesson and may include class participation, individual presentations, individual written assignments, and group presentations. In most blocks, group efforts and class participation account for 40 to 70 percent of the grade.

Student assessments in resident and TASS courses are designed to achieve a range of purposes. The most obvious objective is to assess student learning. Assessments provide incentives for individual effort, not only for getting high grades, but also for personal esteem. Participating in staff groups to prepare planning products and presentations also helps students improve their skills in synthesizing and communicating ideas and interacting with others.

ADL

ADL uses multiple choice tests and individual assignments but does not allow for class participation or collaborative assessments. Therefore, course developers have implemented alternative course activities and mechanisms to assess learning. These include graded multiple-choice or true/false tests that are used to determine class participation grades. After completing the test, the student receives the results and is directed to the sections of the course material corresponding to incorrect answers. If the student does not get a passing grade, he or she can re-take the test up to three times. These tests allow for standardized and systematic measurement of student knowledge. However, students receive only automated feedback and do not benefit from the Socratic-type dialogue that occurs in classroom settings. In addition, the level of learning assessed through these mechanisms is generally limited to knowledge and sometimes comprehension (Bloom, 1956; 1994). A second mechanism used in ADL is for the student to be assigned a portion of a group effort and a related written product, which is performed and graded individually. This approach allows ADL students to work on part of a task in ways that might mirror the division of labor in resident or TASS teams. However, the student does not get the experience of collaborating with others and misses the learning that occurs in developing a broader group product.

Scheduling and Time Requirements

In general, the Common Core is designed to be the same length and to involve comparable work across the venues; however, the actual time spent varies, as shown in Table 2.3. Although course hours (total for both in and out of the classroom) are similar for all three venues (306-307 hours), the time span over which instruction occurs varies significantly (from 16 weeks for resident to up to 18 months for ADL), as do the constraints that the course puts on student time.

Table 2.3. Length and Time Requirements Across Venues

Variable	Resident	TASS	ADL
Class Hours	306	249	0
ADL Hours	0	57	307, but can be far less
Time Period	16 weeks[a]	Typically 12 to 18 months	Up to 18 months
Class Hours/Day	5.38 hours	• 7.1-7.9 classroom hours/day (Phases I and III) • 6 classroom hours/day Phase II)	Individually scheduled
Continuity of Learning	5 days/week while course is in session	• Phase I and III have 11 continuous days (except Sundays) • Phase II is carried out over 8 months, 1 weekend per month	Self-paced, varies
Non-Duty Time Requirements	Some homework	• Phase II ADL lessons (57 hours) and small number of ADL lessons in Phases I and III on non-duty status for many students • An unknown number of students participate in Phase II weekend classes outside of normal duty time or for retirement points • Much more homework outside of normal duty time compared to resident venue	• Completed in an unpaid status for many students (over 60% based on survey responses) • Homework normally unpaid

[a] The resident course is 14 weeks at satellite locations.

Scheduling

Course schedules vary across the three venues. The resident course follows a somewhat predictable schedule, with class approximately five hours per day for five days per week while the course is in session, and a large portion of homework can be done within the eight-hour training day. In addition, in the 2009-2010 academic year, the Fort Leavenworth resident class had 18 guest speakers, which added 72 hours to the class requirement, and resident students have some responsibilities outside of class.[15] Normally, there are no scheduled classes on weekends. In comparison, TASS Phases I and III require about approximately two more hours in the classroom per day than do resident courses; with homework, this means that TASS students spend more time after normal duty hours during each class day. In addition, because the TASS

---

[15] Resident students must attend four hours of training to learn to use Battle Command Systems (BCS), which is used in the classroom, and they remain at school for multiple other administrative and post activities such as unit runs, funerals, physical examinations and training, and other mandatory training (e.g., Operations Security, Prevention of Sexual Harassment).

course is geared toward the RC, students attend weekend classes. Although the Phase I and III students are on Active Duty for Training (ADT) status, which limits family and other obligations after class, the considerable amount of time spent on coursework each day and during ADT as a whole may interfere with learning; substantial research evidence shows that massed practice (e.g., learning that occurs within one time interval with few or limited breaks) inhibits task performance and knowledge retention compared to distributed practice (which occurs in shorter intervals over a longer time period) (Cepeda, 2006; Donovan and Radosevich, 1999).

From a student learning perspective, the weekend Phase II of TASS is even more challenging than the resident course because of the length of the commute required. In contrast to resident course students at Fort Leavenworth who are on permanent change of station (PCS) and reside close to the school, TASS students have to travel, sometimes over long distances, to reach their weekend instructional sites. Phase II weekend schedules also makes staff group integration more difficult. The non-contiguous nature of Phase II could also lead to learning decay. TASS instructors attempt to mitigate these effects by starting weekend sessions with reviews and by encouraging students to interact via email, telephone, and use of SharePoint sites (internal collaboration/document and file management websites), but the extent to which ongoing collaboration occurs during Phase II is unknown.

Although ADL is listed as requiring 306 hours, the amount of time students spend on the course varies. To some extent, the design of the ADL courseware (e.g., required checks on learning) prevents students from "clicking through." However, because the ADL is self-paced and does not include discussion activities, it is possible for ADL students to go through the course content considerably more quickly than students in resident or TASS courses, especially if the ADL students focus on doing the minimum necessary to complete the requirements.

Non-Duty Time Requirements

TASS Phase II and ADL students are required to exert a greater amount of effort outside of normal duty hours than are their resident counterparts. Homework and out-of-class assignments are completed on students' discretionary time for Phase II TASS and the entire ADL course. In addition, anecdotal evidence suggests that some TASS students in Phase II attend the Common Core during a second weekend each month, either in an ADT or on unpaid status, because their unit commander may need their participation in the unit's regular Inactive Duty Training (IDT) weekend activities. Additionally, the data reported in Chapter 3 indicate that the majority of ADL students attend the Common Core on discretionary time. Extra weekends or working on discretionary time means that the course might conflict with full-time jobs and family responsibilities, with the net result being that TASS and ADL students have difficulties devoting the same level of effort to the course as do their resident counterparts. The logical consequence is that many TASS and ADL students will devote less time, with a potential negative impact on learning.

Instructors and Instructor Development

There are a number of differences between resident and TASS instructors. Although ADL does not use facilitated instruction, it does have designated faculty who grade student assignments and contractors who operate the ADL help desk. Table 2.4 summarizes key information about instructors and instructor development across the three venues.

Table 2.4. Instructors and Instructor Development Across Venues

Variable	Resident	TASS	ADL[a]
Personnel Qualifications	• Either Title 10 civilians or active duty officers • Title 10 civilians hired based on skills and experience • Master's degree • Military Education Level 4 (MEL 4)/JPME 1	• USAR officers • Master's degree • MEL 4/JPME 1	• Part-time adjunct faculty and contracted help desk support hired with consideration of relevant experience • Some adjunct faculty RC officers who receive retirement points for grading assessments • AOC blended learning instructors assist as needed
Full/Part-Time	Full time	Part-time 38+ day drilling reservists	Part-time volunteers (often receiving retirement points only)
Generalist/ Specialist	Specialists (assigned to 1 of 5 teaching departments)	Generalists Reserve instructor duty on non-deployable status	Generalists
Term of Service	Military—3 years, but often less; civilian—Title 10 renewable contract	3 to 5 years	Not limited
Formal Development Activities	• Faculty Development Phase 1 (FDP1): ELM • FDP2: Lesson Implementation	• FDP1 at Leavenworth • FDP2 conducted by 97th's chain of command	• Little formal preparation • Must have graduated from CGSOC • FDP1 and FDP2 encouraged, but not required
Informal Development Activities	Extensive but optional (e.g., doctrinal updates, unit training exercises, operations)	Available but limited by number of days reservist has allotted to direct instruction and development	• Faculty can watch video-taped sessions as needed (e.g., FDPs, doctrinal updates).

[a]ADL now has several full-time faculty to mentor and coach students, and these instructors will play an increased role in grading student assignments over time.

Resident

Fort Leavenworth has full-time instructors, about 60 percent of whom are Title 10 civilians, with the remainder being active duty officers. Instructors are specialists assigned to one of the five functional teaching departments (Tactics, Joint/Multinational, Force Management/Logistics,

History, and Leadership) and their instructional responsibilities are in those areas. Resident instructors are organized into multifunctional instructor teams, each with 12 instructors assigned from functional departments. Each team is aligned with four student staff groups throughout the course. Although the goal is for active duty officers to be assigned for three years, the actual length is often less because of operational demands.

Although officers are Department of the Army (DA)-selected, CGSS has some authority to review the officers' records before assignment as well as some latitude in rearranging officer assignments at Fort Leavenworth across organizations. CGSS also has considerable flexibility in selecting Title 10 instructors and has established criteria for filling those positions. Title 10 instructors can serve as long as the requirement remains and they and the CGSS staff desire.

Fort Leavenworth has established formal and informal faculty development programs. The two-week Faculty Development Phase 1 (FDP1) course covers ELM and general teaching skills, and FDP2 focuses on course subject matter content and delivery. Both FDP1 and FDP2 courses provide opportunities for participants to lead blocks of instruction, which are observed by the instructor's senior rater. The department and school also offer informal, but often extensive, internal development programs that can include such activities as doctrine updates, unit training exercises, and deployment on real-world operations.

TASS

TASS instructors are USAR officers who typically serve as instructors for three to five years. However, because they have other careers and a limited amount of funded duty days for instructional duties, they serve less time than do their resident counterparts.[16] Traditionally, a reservist serves 38 plus active days per year; 24 IDT days, typically on weekends, and 13 or more Annual Training (AT) days. A limited number of additional training or support days can be provided, but reservists cannot be required to perform more than their IDT and AT days, and funds for additional days are limited.[17] Qualified officers apply to the 97th's chain of command for selection.

TASS instructors go through the same general faculty development process as do resident instructors and attend the FDP1 at Fort Leavenworth, whereas FDP2 is conducted by the 97th's chain of command. The 97th Brigade sends some of its instructors to Fort Leavenworth's FDP2 programs, and videotapes of Fort Leavenworth FDP2 are available on the Common Core Blackboard content management system for TASS faculty. The 97th Brigade also has informal instructor development programs, but reservists' participation is limited by the number of days they have for direct instruction and development.

---

[16] The USAR also has Army/Guard Reserve (AGR) officers who serve on a full-time status, but the 97th Brigade does not have AGRs serving as instructors.

[17] An RC soldier can also be mobilized and come on active duty full time for the period of mobilization. Currently, the Army does not mobilize reservists to support Common Core instruction.

Compared to resident instructors, TASS instructors tend to be generalists, but their varying backgrounds give course managers some potential for achieving specialization within three-person staff groups (and by having some instructors serve as guest lecturers across staff groups). However, as a part of instructor development, one staff group member is often a new instructor, which limits the ability of the instructors to specialize.

The typical TASS instructor has some developmental constraints compared to the resident instructors. TASS instructors spend less time teaching the course and have less time to develop their CGSOC instructional skills and subject matter expertise. Moreover, TASS instructors have a greater requirement in terms of content in that they generally have to be knowledgeable about a larger number of Common Core lessons than do their Fort Leavenworth counterparts. It is also more convenient for resident instructors at Fort Leavenworth to keep current with changing doctrinal concepts and methods because they are collocated, not only with other instructors and faculty, but also with other Combined Arms Center staff organizations, such as doctrine writers and force development staffs.

ADL

At the time that this research was conducted, ADL had no instructors as such, but relied on part-time adjunct faculty who grade assignments as well as help desk staff to provide technical and course content support to students. Most adjunct faculty are part-time RC officers or retirees. In addition, some full-time AOC instructors grade assignments as needed. Graders do not get paid directly for this work but receive retirement points. There are about 40 adjunct faculty members in this category.

Adjunct faculty have little formal preparation compared to resident instructors. They must have graduated from CGSOC and are encouraged, but are not required, to complete FDP1 or FDP2. Some adjunct faculty are course developers or are otherwise involved in support of CGSOC and therefore are knowledgeable about course content. CGSS also offers informal, elective developmental activities for faculty on topics such as course content and grading.

CGSS has since added several full-time faculty to the ADL program to mentor and coach students. These faculty will play an increased role in grading student assignments over time.

Instructional Support

Table 2.5 compares course materials and facility support available for instructors and students across the three venues.

Table 2.5. Course Materials and Facility Support Across Venues

Variable	Resident	TASS	ADL
Course Materials	• Students—Online readings, case studies, complex operational scenarios • Instructors—Lesson plans, lesson guides, guides for assessing student assignments • Access to informal faculty development opportunities	Same access to materials as resident	Same access to online materials as resident
Facilities	New building and modern facilities, including extensive research facilities	Facilities vary, but are generally adequate	No dedicated facilities or equipment

Course Materials

Resident and TASS instructors have access to a large amount of online course materials, such as detailed lesson plans, lesson guides, and other support materials to assist with their preparation, presentations, and work with students, including links to the lesson authors in case the instructors have questions. There are also extensive guides for assessing student assignments. Students at all venues have access to the same online materials. These resources especially benefit ADL and Phase II TASS students, who often do not have access to learning centers at an installation.

Facility Support

The facilities across ADT and IDT TASS sites vary. The Phase I and III sites, although less modern and complete than those at Fort Leavenworth, are generally equivalent. The Phase II TASS sites vary considerably but are generally adequate.[18] The major advantages for resident faculty are the opportunities for informal development that were discussed earlier. ADL RC adjunct faculty and students have no dedicated facilities or learning centers for CGSOC, and students and graders secure their own hardware, software, and Internet access.

Chapter Conclusion

Table 2.6 summarizes key differences across venues for all categories.

---

[18] Based on input from Combined Arms Center (CAC) Quality Assurance teams.

Table 2.6. Summary of Differences Across Venues

Variable	Resident	TASS	ADL
Instructional approach	ELM (collaborative learning)	ELM (collaborative learning)	IMI (individual learning)
Assessments of student learning	Individual and group	Individual and group	Individual
Course scheduling and time constraints	• Contiguous and completed in about 4 months • Coursework can generally be completed in 8-hour day • Fort Leavenworth students on PCS	• Three phases over 12-18 months • Longer days • More consecutive days in Phases I and III • Phases I and III on ADT; Phase II on alternate IDT, ADT, or discretionary time	• Three phases over 12-18 months • For most students, completed on discretionary time
Instructors and instructor development	• Full-time, 60/40 civilian/military specialists • Extensive formal and informal development	• Part-time, Reserve generalists in non-deployable status • Full formal and limited informal development	• Adjunct generalists (not instructors) used to grade assessments • Limited formal or informal development
Instructional support	• Online course materials for instructors and students • Excellent facilities and equipment support	• Online course materials for instructors and students • Generally equivalent facilities and equipment for Phases I and III; varied for Phase II	• Online materials for students • No facilities • Full-time help desk

Although the learning goals and objectives in resident, TASS, and ADL venues are the same, there is considerable variation in a number of factors across venues. The greatest differences are seen between ADL and the other venues. Compared to the ADL venue, resident instruction has students with greater military experience, more opportunities for collaborative learning and discussion through the use of ELM strategies, fewer constraints on student time, and greater levels of facilitation through instructors with more resources at their disposal. The TASS venue is similar to the resident venue in many ways, particularly in relation to instructional strategies. However, students in the TASS venue tend to have lower levels of operational experience than do resident students as well as competing demands on their time (especially in Phase II), and there are fewer developmental opportunities for instructors.

These differences are substantive enough that they would logically lead to expectations that learning outcomes and student reactions and attitudes about the course will differ among venues. In brief, we would expect the most favorable outcomes in resident training due to greater military experience of AC resident students, the use of ELM strategies and collaborative learning experiences, minimal constraints on student time, and facilitation by instructors with more resources at their disposal.[19] We would expect relatively similar outcomes in TASS and resident venues given that they have many features in common, particularly with respect to instructional strategies. However, outcomes in TASS would logically be somewhat less favorable because of lower levels of students' operational experience, competing demands on students' time (especially in Phase II), and fewer development opportunities for instructors. In contrast, we expect the least favorable outcomes in ADL largely because of the individual learning model in this venue. To the degree that ELM and Socratic methods are important to the acquisition of critical thinking skills, there should be meaningful differences among resident, TASS, and ADL student grades as well as in perceptions of learning and reactions to course design.

These predictions are substantiated by other research (Straus et al., 2013) which asked AOC students to compare their experiences in AOC, which used distributed blended learning, with their experience in the Common Core. Results showed that the venue in which students took the Common Core influenced their perceptions of blended learning, such that students who graduate from the ADL Common Core had more favorable reactions toward AOC, and students who graduated from the resident Common Core had the least favorable reactions to AOC.

As will be seen in the next chapters, however, we did not find the types of differences in learning outcomes and student reactions that we anticipated. We will discuss the possible reasons for this discrepancy in Chapter 3. In addition, we will draw upon the data presented in this chapter to help inform the discussion of student post-training reactions and attitudes and our recommendations for improving the Common Core in each venue.

---

[19]Note, however, that this may not be true for general learning goals, such as effective writing skills or critical thinking, because these are not directly related to specific military experience.

3. STUDENTS' POST-TRAINING REACTIONS AND ATTITUDES

The CGSS evaluation process relies heavily on surveys of students' reactions toward the quality of instructional delivery and attitudes regarding how effectively they achieved course objectives. In this chapter, we describe the surveys that CGSC administered in each venue, present results of analyses of responses to close-ended (i.e., objective) questions, discuss alternative explanations for results, present results of analyses of responses to open-ended questions, and discuss limitations and conclusions.

Student surveys are the most common method of evaluation in training and education. Surveys of learners can be used to measure reactions to numerous aspects of a course, including the quality of course content, design, and delivery, instructor style, and organizational support – thus providing valuable information that can be used to improve course quality (e.g., Sitzmann et al., 2008). Moreover, student reactions can be associated with other evaluation outcomes, including learning and transfer performance (Alliger et al., 1997) and objective measures of learning (Sitzmann et al., 2008) (although such associations are typically modest, e.g., Sitzmann et al., 2010b).

Surveys can also be used to evaluate post-training attitudes reflecting changes in learners, such as self-efficacy and learning motivation (Kraiger, Ford, and Salas, 1993). Sitzmann et al. (2008) found that self-efficacy was strongly related to immediate and delayed procedural knowledge. Such measures can be particularly valuable when it is impractical or difficult to assess learning outcomes (Sitzmann et al., 2008), as is the case with many aspects of the Common Core.

Overview of Results

The surveys are comprehensive, addressing different aspects of students' experiences in the course. Analysis of the survey responses presented below suggest that, on the whole, students in all venues generally felt that the course contributed to their learning and were satisfied with most features of the course, including the quality of assessments (e.g., exams, papers, and other assignments), and the quality of instructional delivery. This suggests that, overall, the Common Core is successful from students' perspectives.

With a few exceptions, we found minimal differences in student reactions across the venues. These results might be used to draw the conclusion that the three modes of delivery are equally effective. However, as we explain below, there are alternative explanations for the results shown. In the latter part of this chapter, we explore the possibility that common biases in responding to surveys may be misrepresenting students' actual experiences in the course. These patterns of responses, in addition to inherent differences in the student populations and structure of resident,

TASS, and ADL venues, make it difficult to draw meaningful conclusions about differences among venues.

Nonetheless, some measures, along with responses to open-ended questions included on the surveys, point to areas where improvements in the course may be needed, such as better and more timely feedback for ADL students and better information technology support and/or training for TASS students. We provide a detailed discussion of improvements in Chapter 5.

Survey Use in the Common Core

Survey Administration

Survey administration varied somewhat for resident instruction compared to TASS and ADL courses. This was, in part, because of inherent differences in course structure and delivery modes among the venues, but also because different organizations within CGSC managed the resident survey and the TASS and ADL surveys.

Because there was a different instructor for each block of the resident course, students completed a survey after each unit of instruction, for a total of nine surveys. In the last three weeks of the course, four surveys were administered in close succession. In contrast, there was one survey at the end of each phase in TASS and ADL venues, for a total of three surveys. These surveys addressed multiple blocks and therefore were substantially longer than most of the surveys administered in the resident course. To reduce response burden, the Phase II survey in TASS and ADL and the Phase III survey in TASS were split into two, and each version was randomly assigned to one half of the students.[20] Surveys were administered online and completed on an anonymous basis.

Survey Content

The resident course is on a different schedule (August to November) than the TASS and ADL courses (May to August), and the surveys in the resident course had already been administered at the outset of this project. Therefore, because CGSS was interested in comparing responses across venues, the resident surveys shaped the content of the TASS and ADL surveys. Survey topics and question formats varied somewhat, however, because of (1) differences in the sequence of topics in each venue, (2) differences in activities and assignments among the venues, (3) survey length – some questions from the resident survey were eliminated or condensed in the TASS and ADL surveys to reduce response burden, and (4) capabilities of the survey software

---

[20] In Phase II, Version 1 had questions about Strategic Environment, History, and Leadership, and Version 2 had questions about Doctrine and Force Management. In Phase III, Version 1 had questions about Joint Functions, and Version 2 had questions about Planning. Therefore, about half of the total respondents answered questions about perceived cognitive learning and the quality of assessments in these blocks. All surveys had questions about instructional delivery.

used in each venue.[21] The number of items per survey ranged from 64 to 74 in ADL, 46 to 69 in TASS, and 28 to 60 in resident. Appendixes B and C include examples of the survey items.

There were five general categories of survey questions:

- Post-training attitudes regarding cognitive learning. These items asked students to assess whether they achieved a variety of learning objectives or whether they felt that they learned the substantive material in the course. (A typical item was, "C100 improved my knowledge of the Army Leader Development Process.")
- Student reactions regarding the adequacy of assignments and exams as valid measures of their knowledge (e.g., "The C200 examination accurately tested my analysis of U.S. Defense Strategy").
- Student reactions regarding the quality of instructional delivery. Each survey in the resident course had a standard set of questions, referred to in CGSC as "classroom environment," as well as other questions about readings and assignments. All TASS surveys asked the same questions about instructional delivery. In the ADL surveys, these questions were adapted for the medium. For example, the resident and TASS surveys included an item, "Classroom discussions encouraged critical thinking." In the ADL survey, this item was revised as "The ADL lessons encouraged critical thinking." In resident surveys, these questions were asked for each block, and in TASS and ADL surveys they were asked for each phase.
  - o At RAND's recommendation, the ADL and TASS surveys also included other items about instructional delivery. ADL surveys in Phases I and II included questions about the technical features of the courseware, as did the TASS Phase II survey, since ADL lessons were used to deliver History and Leadership blocks of instruction.[22] The TASS and ADL surveys also included questions assessing overall satisfaction (Straus et al., 2011). The surveys included other items, e.g., about the course readings or level of difficulty of the course, but use of these questions was not systematic across venues or Phases. We discuss these responses where relevant.
- Open-ended questions about each block of instruction and a final question asking for any other comments.
- Student demographic characteristics in the ADL and TASS surveys, but these questions varied by Phase and/or venue.

---

[21] Inquisite software, which was used to administer the resident survey, allows for questions in table format in which the "stem" of a question can be presented once, followed by multiple options. The version of Blackboard that was used to administer the survey in ADL and TASS did not have this functionality, so that the stem had to be repeated in each question.

[22] These questions were eliminated from the ADL Phase 3 survey, as the data from the earlier phases indicated that few ADL students had technical difficulties.

Most items about learning and instructional delivery had five-point Likert-type response options, ranging from strongly agree to strongly disagree with a "neutral" or "neither agree nor disagree" midpoint, although some items had other options such as "yes" or "no."

Response Rates

The number of respondents and response rates for each survey are presented in Tables 3.1 and 3.2. Response rates for resident surveys are based on the number of students who completed the course ($n = 1,054$). Response rates for TASS and ADL surveys are based on the number of students who completed the phase, which varied by phase. Responses to the TASS Phase I survey were excluded from analyses because there was a substantial lag in fielding the survey, resulting in an extremely low response rate and potential problems in recall.

Table 3.1. Response Rates for Surveys in Resident Course

Respondents	Survey								
	C100	C200	C300	C400	C500	C600	L100	H100	F100
Number	436	394	459	459	416	450	398	470	374
Response rate	29%	41%	37%	44%	40%	43%	38%	46%	36%

Table 3.2. Response Rates for Surveys in TASS and ADL Courses

Venue	Respondents	Survey		
		Phase I	Phase II	Phase III
TASS	**Number**	35	455	112
	Response rate	4%	29%	12%
ADL	**Number**	208	117	51
	Response rate	40%	29%	15%

Analyses

Items with strongly agree to strongly disagree response options were scored so that more unfavorable responses (e.g., strongly disagree) were scored as "1" and more favorable responses (e.g., strongly agree) were scored as "5." Responses to items about related topics were combined into scales. Appendixes B and C present the scales corresponding to each block of instruction, number of items on the scales in each venue, and coefficient alpha statistics.[23] Coefficient alpha

---

[23] *Coefficient alpha* is a measure of internal consistency or reliability among a set of items. It typically ranges from zero to one, with higher values indicating greater reliability. Coefficient alpha is influenced by the number of items on a scale; thus, a scale with a few items will typically have a lower alpha than a scale with many items. Coefficient

was high for virtually all scales, with most alphas ranging from 0.77 to 0.94, indicating that respondents were internally consistent.

We report comparisons among venues on comparable items or scales. There were some differences in the wording of some items among venues; therefore, we conducted comparisons only when, in our judgment, these differences did not influence the substantive meaning of the questions. For most comparisons, we analyzed items in common to all surveys. In some cases, a single, general item was used in ADL or TASS, which compared the mean response of multiple, specific questions in resident. Comparisons were conducted using analysis of variance (ANOVA), *t*-tests, and chi-square (χ^2) tests.[24]

In addition, in TASS and ADL venues, we analyzed items that were exclusive to these venues, and we examined the association of demographic characteristics and survey responses.

Results

We report results regarding students' perceptions of the following topics:

- Cognitive learning
- Quality of assessments and exams
- Quality of instructional delivery.

Perceived Cognitive Learning

Figure 3.1 shows students' ratings of the extent to which they felt that they achieved the learning objectives. This figure shows results for a sample of measures from Phase II. Results for questions in Phases I and III are similar and can be found in Appendix D. Examples of the items on each scale and explanations for the abbreviated terms shown in Figures 3.1 and 3.2 can be found in Appendix B.

Results indicate that students felt that they met the learning goals for all blocks. There were some statistically significant differences among venues, but the effect sizes were typically quite small, indicating limited practical significance of these differences.[25] Thus, students in all

---

alpha is not applicable for topics in which items used categorical responses (e.g., yes/no; male/female) or for topics for which there was a single item (e.g., expectations about ADL).

[24] ANOVA and *t*-tests are used for continuous measures to determine whether the means of different groups are equal. *t*-tests are used when two groups are being compared; ANOVA is used for comparison of more than two groups. χ^2 tests are used to analyze whether distributions of categorical variables are different across groups.

[25] Effect sizes estimate the strength of the relationship between variables, in contrast to significance levels, which reflect the probability that the observed relationship could have occurred by chance. When sample sizes are large, as they were for many of the analyses conducted in this study, a statistical test is likely to show a significant difference, even if the size of the test statistic (e.g., a correlation of 0.10) is too small to be considered practically important. According to Cohen (1988), for correlations, an effect size of 0.10 is considered small, 0.30 is medium, and 0.5 is large. A phi (ϕ) coefficient is a type of correlation that indicates the effect size associated with a χ^2 test. For *t*-tests, an effect size (Cohen's *d*) of 0.2 is considered small, 0.5 is medium, and 0.8 is large. For ANOVA, an effect size (η^2) of 0.0099 is considered small, 0.0588 is medium, and 0.1379 is large.

venues generally had similar perceptions about their levels of learning, and all blocks were perceived as beneficial.

Figure 3.1. Perceived Cognitive Learning in Phase II Across Venues

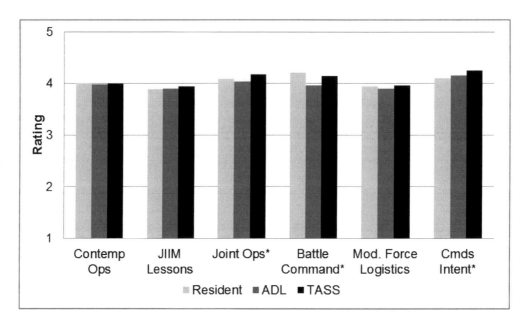

$^*p < 0.05$

Perceived Quality of Assignments and Exams

Students in all venues appear to be generally satisfied with exams and assignments. Figure 3.2 shows ratings of perceived quality of course assessments across venues. Results show statistically significant differences by venue for all but one assignment (the History argumentative essay). However, with the exception of the Strategic Environment assessment, which had a medium effect (Cohen's $d = 0.41$), effect sizes for the differences in venues were small, indicating no practical significance of these differences.

Figure 3.2. Perceived Quality of Assessments Across Venues

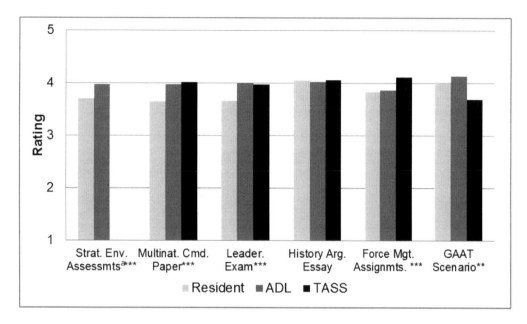

NOTE: GAAT is Georgia-Armenia-Azerbaijan-Turkey.
[a]As noted earlier, responses for TASS Phase I were eliminated because of the low response rate.

$**p < 0.01, ***p < 0.001$

Perceived Quality of Instructional Delivery

Figures 3.3 through 3.5 show students' ratings of instructional delivery. Results for the resident course depicted in the figures are based on weighted averages across blocks corresponding to the Phases in ADL and TASS (Foundations and Strategic Environment in Phase I, JIIM Capabilities, Doctrine, History, Leadership, and Force Management in Phase II, and Joint Functions and Planning in Phase III). Average ratings of the individual blocks in the resident course were high, ranging from 4.2 to 4.5.

Students gave favorable ratings of instructional delivery in all venues. The effect size indicates that the differences among venues in Phase I was not practically significant; in Phase II, the effect size was small to medium ($\eta^2 = 0.035$). There were no differences across venues in Phase III.

Figure 3.3. Ratings of Instructional Delivery in Resident, ADL, and TASS Venues

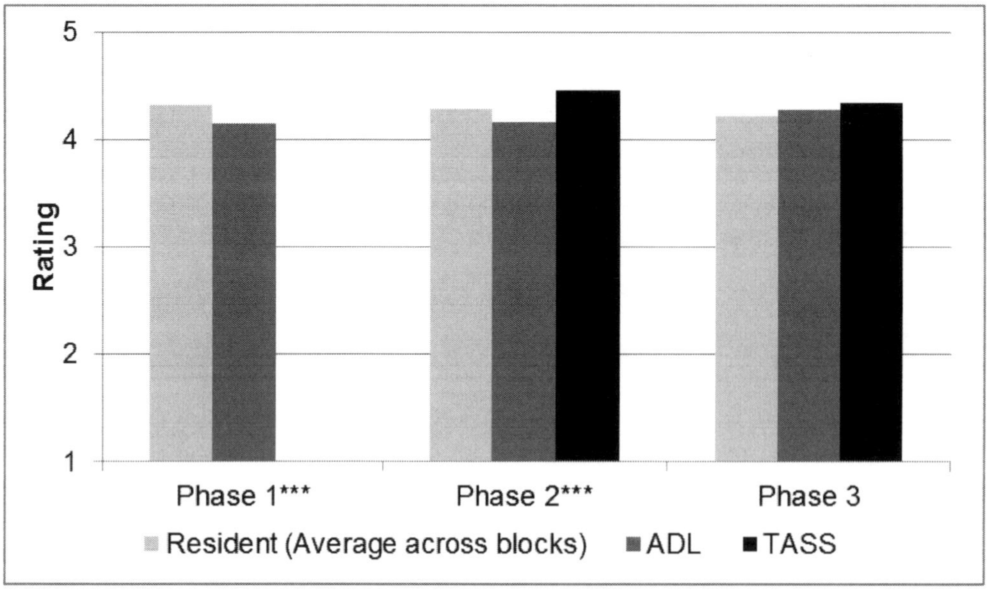

***p < 0.001

Results were similar for most of the individual items in this scale, including appropriateness of technology use, the extent to the which the lessons (ADL) or instructor (TASS and resident) stimulated critical thinking, and the degree to which the lessons (ADL) or class discussions (TASS and resident) provided examples to enhance learning. Results were also similar for comparisons of TASS students' ratings of the quality of ADL lessons and ADL students' ratings of those same items.

However, ratings of the perceived value of course feedback differed by venue. As shown in Figure 3.4, ratings of the extent to which feedback enhanced student learning were lower in ADL compared to resident in Phase I (data for TASS were not available) and compared to both resident and TASS in Phase II.[26] Resident students' ratings were also lower than those given by TASS students. The effect size was small to medium ($\eta^2 = 0.047$); however, given the relatively high ratings on most survey items in ADL, this difference is striking. There were no differences in perceptions of feedback quality among venues in Phase III; this is likely because there were few gradable assignments in this phase.[27]

---

[26] Contrasts between ADL and the other venues were as follows: In Phase I, $F(1) = 25.82$, $p < 0.001$; in Phase II, $F(1) = 67.92$, $p < 0.001$; in Phase III, $F(1) = 2.84$, $p < 0.10$.

[27] Ratings of the timeliness of feedback, which were measured in ADL Phases II and III and TASS Phase II, were similar to those for feedback quality.

Figure 3.4. Ratings of Feedback Quality in Resident, ADL, and TASS Venues

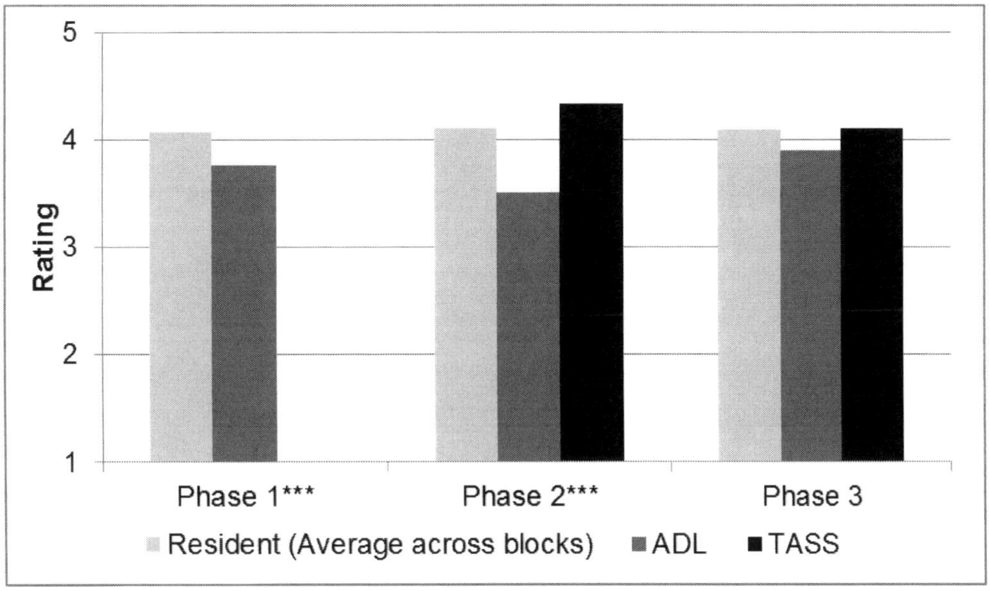

***$p < 0.001$

ADL students' ratings of overall course satisfaction differed from those of TASS students. There were some items about the course that were administered only in TASS and ADL venues. Figure 3.5 shows students' rating of overall satisfaction with the course. This scale consisted of two items, "Overall, I was satisfied with the Phase [ ] course" (referred to "general satisfaction" below), and "I would recommend this course to others." Results show that ADL students' ratings differed in all three phases, with the highest ratings in Phase I and the lowest ratings in Phase II, whereas TASS students' ratings were stable from Phase II to Phase III.[28] The effect size ($\eta^2 = 0.23$) was large, indicating that the results are practically significant. In Phases II and III, ADL students' ratings were also significantly lower than ratings in TASS, with large effect sizes.[29]

We also analyzed the two items on this scale separately, because internal consistency reliability was somewhat low for this scale in Phase III (alpha = 0.60) and was lower in ADL than in TASS. In Phase III, ADL students were much less likely than TASS students to report that they would recommend the course to others. There were smaller differences among venues in general satisfaction with the course.[30]

---

[28] For ADL students' ratings across phases, $F(2,362) = 54.20$, $p < 0.001$. For TASS students' ratings in Phases II and III, $t(193.69) < 1$.

[29] Cohen's $d = 0.89$ and 0.81, respectively.

[30] For recommending the course to others, the average rating was 3.84 in ADL and 4.59 in TASS ($t(72.68) = -4.97$, $p < 0.001$, Cohen's $d = 0.9$). For the item measuring general satisfaction, the average rating was 4.02 in ADL and 4.32 in TASS ($t(159) = -2.46$, $p < 0.05$, Cohen's $d = 0.42$).

Figure 3.5. Ratings of Overall Satisfaction in ADL and TASS Venues

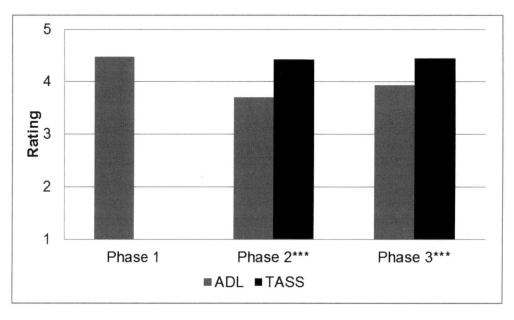

***$p < 0.001$

Ratings of lower satisfaction in ADL were surprising in light of students' consistently high ratings of other aspects of the course. Ratings of satisfaction were not associated with demographic characteristics that were measured in the surveys, as described in more detail below. It is not clear why students in ADL reported lower levels of overall satisfaction with the course than TASS students did, or why ADL students reported being generally satisfied with the course but were less inclined to recommend the course to others.[31]

Responses to a question administered in the Phase III survey are consistent with these results. Students were asked if they had a choice to complete Phase III through online or in-class instruction, which venue they would choose. As shown in Figure 3.6, ADL students were evenly split between online or in-class options, whereas TASS students overwhelmingly selected in-class instruction.[32]

---

[31] Satisfaction was highly correlated with many of the other scales in the survey for both TASS and ADL students, so it is not clear what is driving lower ratings in ADL. We did not find recurrent themes in responses to open-ended questions for students who reported lower satisfaction in Phase II.

[32] $\chi^2_{(1)} = 55.57, p < 0.001, \phi = 0.59$.

Figure 3.6. Future Media Choices for Phase 3 Among ADL and TASS Students

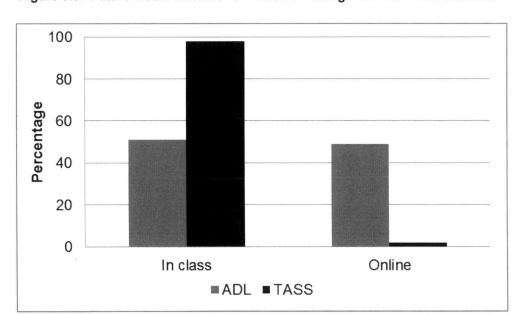

Both TASS and ADL students reported technical and administrative problems with ADL lessons. Figure 3.7 depicts the percentage of students who reported difficulties with technical and/or administrative aspects of the ADL lessons in ADL Phases I and II and in TASS Phase II.[33,34] Not surprisingly, the percentage of students reporting problems was lower in ADL than in TASS, presumably because ADL students have more experience with the courseware and, in some cases, they signed up for ADL because they preferred online learning.[35] It is somewhat surprising, however, that the percentage of students reporting problems in ADL did not decrease for most issues from Phase I to Phase II. This result may have occurred, in part, because some students switched between TASS and ADL, resulting in students in ADL Phase II who were less experienced with the courseware.

As shown in Figure 3.7, more than 15 percent of TASS respondents report needing support for a number of technical issues with the courseware. For ADL students, the technical issues most in need of attention included problems registering for the course and submitting assignments. (Note that the question about registration was asked only following Phase I, and the question about submitting assignments was asked only for ADL students. In addition, registration for the course occurs through the Army Training Requirements and Resource System – ATRRS – not through CGSC). Rates were somewhat lower for difficulties accessing the courseware over the Internet; playing audio, video, or animations in the course; and returning to

---

[33] Questions were omitted from ADL Phase 3 because of low frequencies for most technical and administrative aspects of the course.

[34] Effect sizes were small to medium for statistically significant differences.

[35] The association of preferences for online learning and other variables is reported later in this chapter.

the spot where the student left off after exiting the software ("continue lesson"). Fewer ADL students reported problems with having access to a reliable computer, navigating through the courseware, or getting answers to questions about course content. Note, however, that response options for these questions were "yes" and "no" and therefore do not indicate if these problems created meaningful barriers to completing the ADL lessons.

Figure 3.7. Percentage of ADL and TASS Students Reporting Technical and/or Administrative Difficulties

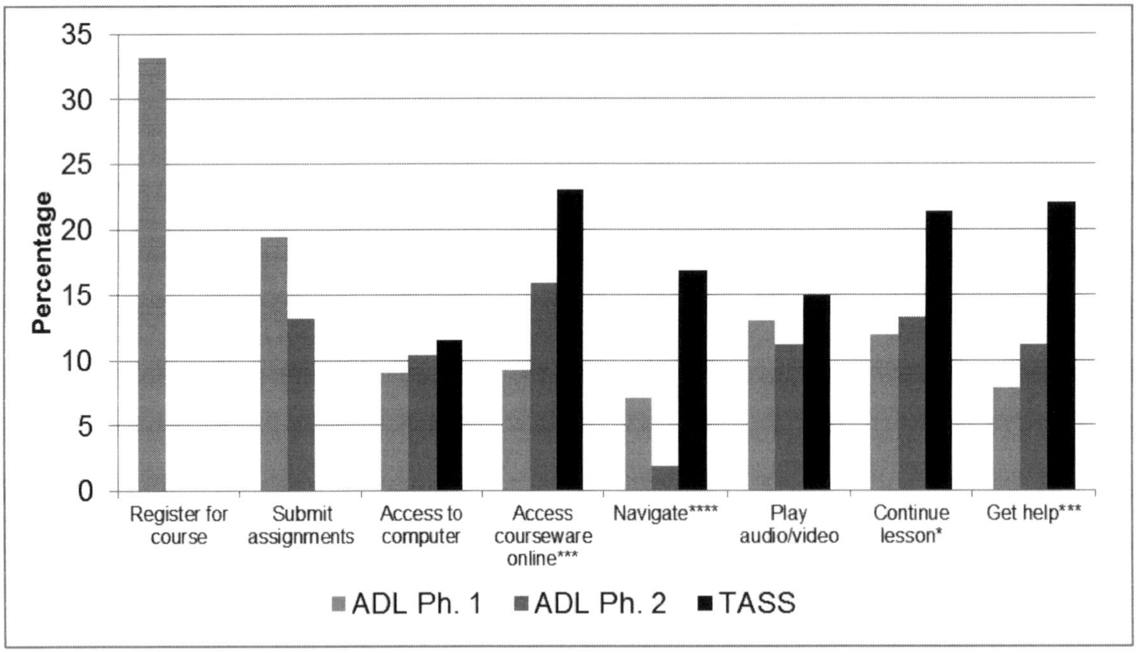

*p < 0.05, ***p < 0.001

There were some measures collected consistently only in the ADL surveys:

- The average rating of an item regarding whether students were fully informed of what was expected of them as an ADL student was 3.26 (standard deviation, SD, = 0.79) in Phase I and 3.46 (SD = 1.07) in Phase II. In comparison to responses to many of the other survey measures, this suggests that many students were not fully aware of what was involved in taking the online course.[36]
- ADL students provided only moderate endorsement of online collaborative tools. Responses to an item about whether online collaborative tools would enhance their learning show average ratings of 3.26 (SD = 0.79) in Phase I and 3.24 (SD = 0.96) in Phase II.
- As shown in Figure 3.8, most students felt that the level of difficulty of Phases I and III were "about right," although students were split between "about right" and "too difficult"

---

[36] Inaccurate or unrealistic expectations about the course may account for lower satisfaction in ADL compared to TASS, but there are other factors that could also explain this difference.

for Phase II. We surmise that these differences between phases occurred because Phase II is much more labor intensive, but this is conjecture, and the survey responses do not allow us to diagnose the reasons for these responses.

Figure 3.8. Perceived Difficulty of Phases in ADL

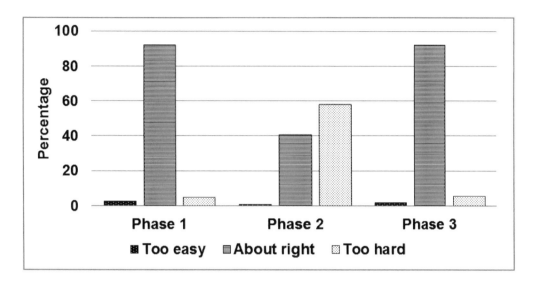

Association of Individual Characteristics and Survey Ratings

The ADL surveys and TASS Phase III collected data regarding demographic characteristics and other contextual factors for students taking the course, although some of variables collected varied by phase. We examined the extent to which students' component, career field, payment status while taking the course (i.e., whether students were completing the course on duty time and thus getting paid, personal time, or a combination of the two), and reasons for taking the Common Core online were associated with ratings of course objectives, course assignments and activities, and instructional design. We summarize these results here; a more detailed description of results, as well as descriptive statistics of individual characteristics, are reported in Appendix E.

There were few associations between students' demographic characteristics and survey responses. We found few associations between component or career field and survey responses. Not surprisingly, students who reported that they prefer learning in an online environment (either as the sole reason for taking ADL or in combination with other reasons) had more favorable evaluations of many aspects of the course than did other students. However, only a very small percentage of students in ADL were predisposed to online learning. It is somewhat surprising that in comparison to other groups, these students did not have more favorable ratings of the potential value of online collaboration tools. There was only one effect for payment status: Students who reported working on their own time gave lower ratings of the quality of instructional delivery compared to students who were on duty status or who worked equal amounts of duty time and personal time.[37] Given the large number of statistical tests, this result could have occurred by chance.

The lack of association of payment status and other survey responses is surprising, given prior research findings showing a negative association of working on personal time and course outcomes (Straus et al., 2011) and because we would expect students working on discretionary time to find it more difficult to devote sufficient time to the course. Non-significant associations of demographic and contextual variables with measures of attitudes and reactions could be the result of limited variation in survey responses in general; we discuss possible reasons for the lack of variation next.

Alternative Explanations for Results and Data Limitations

In general, students' ratings of most aspects of the Common Core were quite favorable. Although ADL students gave lower ratings on some measures, particularly for aspects of instructional delivery, the mean ratings for ADL students were still high, and most effect sizes were small.

These results might be used to draw the conclusion that the three modes of instructional delivery are equally effective in terms of student perceptions. There are, however, a number of alternative explanations for these results. First, we explored the possibility that common biases in responding to surveys might be masking or otherwise misrepresenting differences among venues. Next, we discuss other factors that pose possible threats to conducting valid comparisons of venues. We also discuss other limitations in the survey data that hinder our ability to conduct comparative analyses. Taken together, these results point to the need for caution in using the survey data to compare results across venues and indicate the need for modifications in evaluation instruments or processes.

Biases

There are several types of biases that could account for the observed patterns of survey responses. Common response biases include leniency bias (excessively positive ratings), severity bias (excessively harsh ratings), and central tendency bias (excessive use of the midpoint of the scale). Leniency, severity, and central tendency can be diagnosed, in part, by excessive use of high, low, and middle or neutral responses, respectively. For all items in the survey using 5-point "strongly agree" to "strongly disagree," we calculated the percentage of students' responses in each category, e.g., the percentage of ones, twos, threes, fours, and fives across all items.

---

[37] $F(2,103) = 3.67, p < 0.05$. The mean rating for the quality of instructional delivery for students working on personal time was 4.08 ($SD = 0.56$), compared to 4.36 ($SD = 0.57$) and 4.37 ($SD = 0.29$) for students on duty time or a mix of duty and personal time, respectively. The effect size for this result was medium ($\eta^2 = 0.07$).

Figure 3.9 shows the average percentage of responses in each response option category for three of the surveys: resident C400 (Doctrine), ADL Phase I, and TASS Phase 2. For example, in the resident C400 survey, on average, approximately 2 percent of responses across all items were rated a "1," 3 percent were rated a "2," 12 percent were rated a "3," 58 percent were rated a "4," and 25 percent were rated a "5." We would not expect severity or central tendency biases given the favorable ratings for most survey items, and this was confirmed by the minimal use of "1's", "2's," and "3's." **The high percentage of "4's" and "5's" could indicate that students were highly satisfied with virtually all aspects of the course; however, it could be an indication of leniency bias.**

Figure 3.9. Average Percentage of Each Rating Across All Survey Items

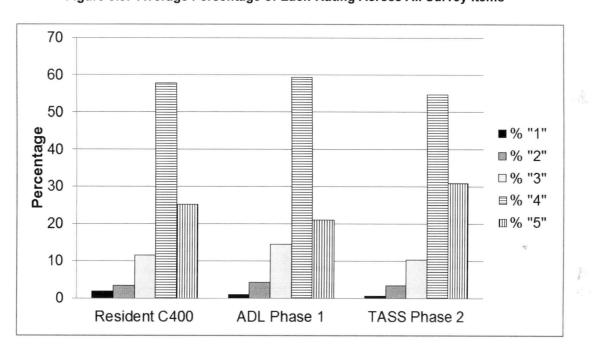

The patterns of responses also suggest a combination of high levels of satisfaction or leniency bias coupled with careless responding, e.g., giving limited thought when answering the questions. We suspected careless responding given the number and length of surveys as well as the level of detail in the majority of the questions. One of many examples consists of questions about JOPP lessons in the C600 (Planning) survey, which asked about 12 objectives, such as comprehending the operational situation, understanding the commander's intent, deducing essential tasks, and developing a clear mission statement. We questioned whether students would be able to recall such specific aspects of the lessons accurately or, alternatively, whether they would have a more general sense of what they learned about a particular topic and therefore would give the same rating to each of detailed questions about that topic.

Careless responding can be signaled in a number of ways, such as short response times, excessive missing data (particularly near the end of a long survey), or strings of the same rating across items (particularly across items measuring different concepts or across negatively and positively worded items). Data about response times to the surveys were not available.

There is some evidence that students gave strings of the same rating throughout the surveys. Figure 3.10 below shows the percentage of students giving the same response (e.g., all ones, all twos) across all items in the survey that used a 5-point agree/disagree scale. This analysis was conducted for three of the resident surveys corresponding to the beginning (C100), middle (C400), and end (C600) of the course. Results suggest patterns of careless responding, and moreover, that this pattern increased over time. For example, 6 percent and 7 percent of students gave the same response to every item on the C100 and C400 surveys, respectively, but 21 percent of students gave the same response to every question on the C600 survey.

Figure 3.10. Percentage of Resident Students Giving the Same Rating Across Survey Items as the Course Progresses

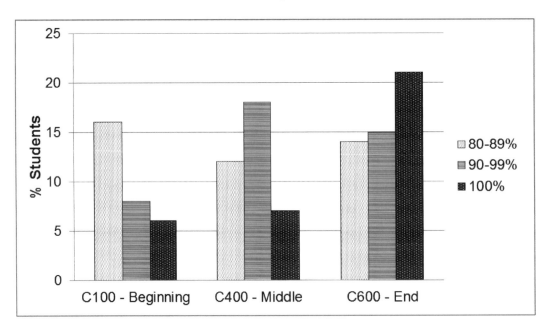

There was also evidence of careless responding or survey fatigue in the ADL and TASS surveys. For example, in the ADL Phase II survey (Part I), there were significantly more missing responses to the second half of the survey (17.4 percent missing, on average) in comparison to the first half (12.2 percent missing, on average) ($t(47) = -6.58$, $p < 0.001$, Cohen's $d = 1.72$). Likewise, evaluation of some of the other surveys shows a larger percentage of missing

38

responses in the second half of the survey.[38] Finally, the drop in response rates shown in Table 3.2 may be another indication of survey fatigue in ADL and TASS.

These results suggest that students are being "over-surveyed" in terms of the number of surveys (particularly in the resident course) and the length of surveys (particularly in TASS and ADL). **Potential negative consequences of excessive requests to complete surveys, including low response rates, incomplete data, and cursory responses, are all evident in the data collected for the Common Core.** As a result, the survey participants may not be representative of the broad population of Common Core students, the responses may not reflect the true sentiments of the students, and the ratings yield limited value for diagnosing problems or identifying areas for improvement.

Threats to Validity

In addition to problems of response biases, there are common threats to validity that render comparisons among venues ambiguous. An obvious issue, common in many studies comparing DL and classroom instruction, is selection bias, i.e., differences in characteristics of students who enrolled in each venue. For example, the majority of students in the resident course were in the AC, whereas most students in TASS and ADL were in the RC. Students in each component may have different experiences with and/or views of the course. Similarly, there may be differences in students who chose to complete the surveys and those who did not; however, we cannot ascertain whether differential selection occurred without knowing the characteristics of students who did and who did not participate. Demand characteristics are another issue, i.e., students may have different expectations for the course depending on the venue in which they were enrolled. For example, because the ADL course has no instructor or peer interaction, students may have had lower expectations for what they would learn, and they adjusted their ratings of the course accordingly. The high ratings observed from ADL students could reflect that the course was good given what they expected.

Other Limitations in the Survey Data

There are a variety of other limitations in the survey data that hamper comparisons across venues or across surveys within venues. First, responses may not be independent across surveys because the same students may have participated in multiple surveys. Analyses cannot control for these dependencies because participation was anonymous. Nonetheless, we recommend maintaining anonymous participation for some measures of reactions to the course in the future to obtain candid responses from the students.

---

[38] In the ADL Phase I survey, there was an average of 6.19 percent missing responses in the first half and 6.98 percent missing responses in the second half ($t(59) = -3.25$, $p < 0.01$). Although the difference in these percentages may seem small, this effect size was large (Cohen's $d = 0.84$). For TASS Phase II Part I survey, the percentages of missing responses were 7.6 percent and 8.1 percent, in the first and second halves of the survey, respectively ($t(63) = -2.34$, $p < 0.05$, Cohen's $d = 0.5$).

Second, there was a lack of consistency in some measures across surveys, both within and among venues. In some cases, this occurred by design, e.g., to reduce response burden in the ADL and TASS surveys, a subset of the detailed questions from the resident surveys were asked or were replaced with one global question. This meant that we could not always compare responses on identical items across venues, although we do not see this as a serious issue, particularly given that students' answers to the detailed questions were highly internally consistent (they tended to give the same answer to items within each scale), and comparisons among venues using individual items from the resident survey were consistent with those using the full scales. In other cases, questions were excluded from one survey or another for unknown reasons. For example, questions about course difficulty and payment status were omitted from the TASS surveys, which meant that we could not conduct potentially useful comparisons within and among venues.

Third, there were problems with survey data preparation in that responses to some questions were not presented and/or coded consistently, for example, with response options for the same item presented in a different order and scored differently across surveys (strongly agree = 1 to strongly disagree = 5 in some surveys and the reverse direction in other surveys). These and other coding inconsistencies were resolved in our analyses, but these discrepancies could have been missed. If CGSS plans to compare responses across venues or across phases within a venue in the future, parallel survey construction and coding will facilitate such analyses.

Responses to Open-Ended Questions

All the surveys included open-ended questions that gave students the opportunity to comment on specific blocks or provide general comments about the course. Below we present results of analysis of responses to the "general comments" questions (typically the last question in each survey) for ADL and TASS in Phase II. We analyzed comments by coding them into one or more of the following categories and by classifying each remark as positive or negative:[39]

- general comments (e.g., "Good course")
- quality of instructional material
- appropriateness of delivery mode
- quality of instructors
- value of classroom interaction
- timing/speed/structure of the course
- value of assignments
- quality or timeliness of feedback

---

[39] An additional category, job relevance of the course, was eliminated because of low frequencies of comments about this topic. Positive comments about job relevance were provided by TASS (but not ADL) students in response to the open-ended question about L100.

- support/administration, e.g., difficulty finding materials
- technical aspects
- course difficulty
- concerns about time or travel to participate
- other.

In the following section, we summarize findings regarding these categories of student feedback and give examples of student comments. Our analysis is not intended to be exhaustive, but instead to provide an example of how this rich data source might be used to address some of the specific questions of interest in this study.

Overview of Open-Ended Responses

Figure 3.11 shows the percentage of students in ADL and TASS who answered the final open-ended question in the Phase II surveys and the nature of their comments. A substantial number of students in each venue (over half of the students) provided one or more comments.

Figure 3.11. Percentage of Comments by Category in ADL and TASS

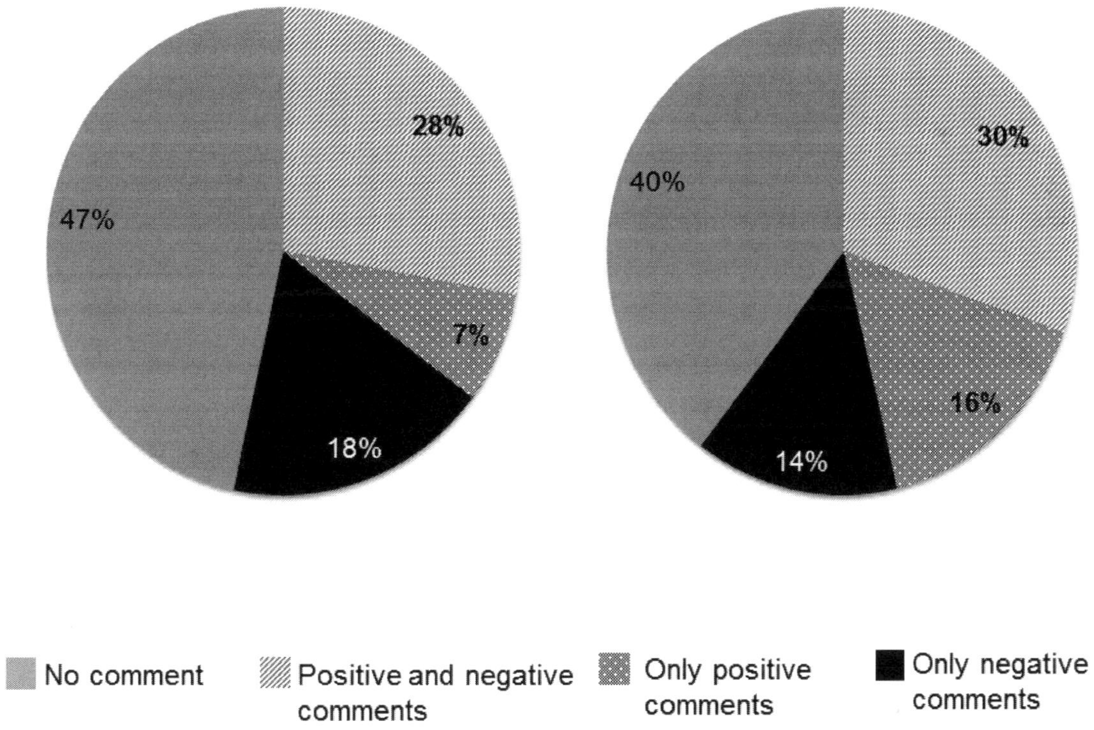

No comment   Positive and negative comments   Only positive comments   Only negative comments

41

Many of the students who answered the question wrote extensive comments that addressed multiple topics. Figures 3.12 and 3.13 show the number of positive and negative comments about specific categories.[40,41] The responses show:

- In TASS, there were numerous positive comments and few negative ones about the course in general as well as about the value of class interaction. Delivery mode and instructors had relatively large numbers of positive and negative comments.
- In ADL, most of the positive comments were general, e.g., "Course was informative and well designed" and "This course has enhanced my military and civilian professional career, great course."
- Categories with the most negative comments (and few positive ones) in TASS included technical aspects and time/travel issues, followed by timing/speed/structure of the course, support/administration, and course difficulty.
- Categories with the highest frequency of negative comments in ADL were timing/speed/structure, followed by feedback and delivery mode.

Figure 3.12. Number of Positive and Negative Comments by Topic in ADL Phase II

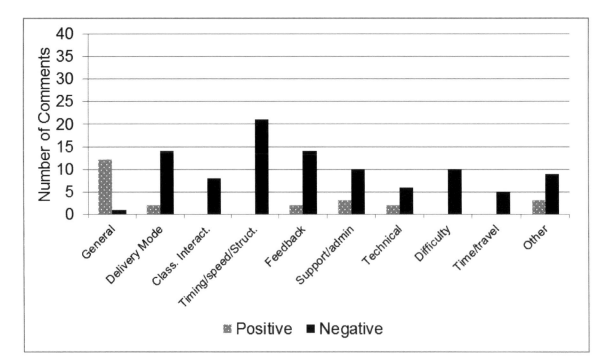

---

[40] We present the number rather than the percentage because many students commented on multiple aspects of the course. In comparison to TASS, there was a smaller number of comments in ADL because there were fewer students who had completed the course when these data were collected.

[41] "Instructional materials," "Assignments," and "Instructors" were eliminated for ADL because of very low frequencies of comments about these topics.

Figure 3.13. Number of Positive and Negative Comments by Topic in TASS Phase II

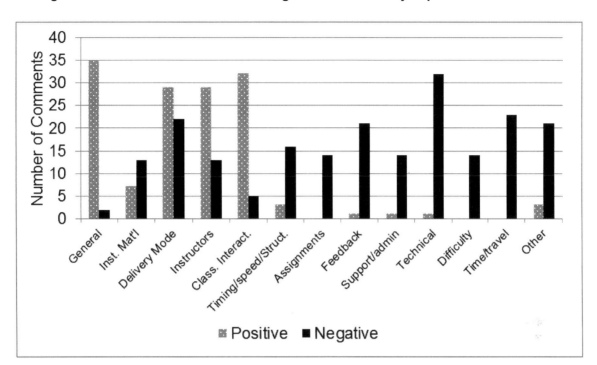

Using Open-Ended Responses to Understand Student Reactions to the Course and Suggestions for Improvement

The open-ended responses are useful for helping understand students' reactions to the course and responses to the survey in more detail. For example, as discussed earlier (Figure 3.4), ADL students gave lower ratings to the value of instructor feedback compared to resident students in Phase I (data for TASS were not available) and compared to both resident and TASS students in Phase II.

Comments made via the open-response field point to sources of students' dissatisfaction with feedback received, particularly for ADL students (the student's venue is noted in parentheses). Among the issues noted are a lack of useful or timely feedback, a preponderance of negative feedback, and uncertainty about what the graders were looking for:

> I often received instructor feedback with nothing but the generic score.... (ADL)

> Getting nothing but negative feedback about assignments for my efforts with no opportunity to improve has me strongly regretting spending all the time I did on this course.... (ADL)

> Better feedback on papers (to include papers with grades above 90). As a DL student it is difficult to get a feel for what the graders are looking for. (ADL)

43

In several instances, especially with guidance on papers, it was very difficult to impossible to receive guidance. (ADL)

The actual classes give examples of the things expected to be drafted such as the commander's intent and commanders tactical problem. The online version does not. It was extremely difficult to discern what it should look like or contain. (ADL)

I was unable to ever receive the actual papers back. This made it difficult to make improvement. I often received instructor feedback with nothing but the generic score. Would be more helpful to see the comments on the paper. If I can scan it in and send, it can be scanned in and returned. (ADL)

Graders who take more than 14 days to grade a paper is unacceptable and is only delaying the student. (ADL)[42]

Feedback from written papers needs to be completed in a more timely manner. (TASS)

The papers and assignments need to be returned to the student quicker. I would have wanted to see the instructor comments on my first paper before I wrote the next month's [paper]. This would have given me the feedback needed to make adjustments as necessary. (TASS)

Some instructors were better than others when it came to grading papers; meaning, they provided more feedback and guided me to what they were trying to pull out of me. Others graded on a PhD scale at which there was nobody in the class that had a PhD. The course work load is already heavy and adding on multiple redos seemed to become counterproductive to the learning process. (TASS)

A related issue mentioned by several students pertained to a lack of consistency in the criteria used for graded assignments:

There is no uniformity in the assignments. Some of them ask for double spaced, new times roman, font 11 answers and some ask for double spaced, one inch margins, new times roman font 12. And God forbid I should have the font wrong

---

[42] Subsequent addition of online drop boxes may have resolved some of the issues with the lack of timely feedback reported by ADL students.

or the margins wrong on the paper I hand in because if I do it is handed back to me and told I have to redo it. (TASS)

Why not make all assignments one-inch margins, Times New Roman, 12 point type (number of pages can vary). There were several assignments that required 11 point type. I humbly encourage you to adapt the old Army style of uniformity when it comes to the assignments. (ADL)

Responses to open-ended questions can also be used to identify suggestions for improving the course. Some of the comments above point to ways to improve feedback, for example, by providing more detailed remarks and by grading papers in a more timely way.

Students provided suggestions regarding a variety of other topics as well. For example, numerous TASS students commented on the amount of work required in Phase II and several recommended changing this phase to a two-week block. While lack of compensation is an underlying issue in a small number of these comments, there are some **pervasive themes in these responses including stress due to role conflict and negative consequences of the workload on educational outcomes.** Some of these comments included suggestions for improvement:

Too much, too fast. All great material, but I fear for my retention.

There is so much information that is required of the student to read that it is virtually impossible to absorb any of it. It is simply read it and get through it so I can get done with this class.

Would have like [SIC] to have all reading material available in audio format. I could have listened to much of the required readings throughout the course if I could play them on my way to and from work every day in my car. The lack of audio files for the reading required me to devote additional time to readings, time much better used by focusing on the actual assignments.

It was difficult for me to complete the class assignments and follow along with the class material and learning requirements during my time in phase II because of my full-time job and other family requirements. Phase II should be delivered in a 2- or 3-week block so that students could concentrate fully on learning.

I believe I would have gotten more out of the resident course because I would have been able to focus more time on the lessons without too many distractions. Maybe the second course can be offered as a two-week course like Phase 1 and 3?

Consolidate the eight weekends into a two-week period of instruction. Eight weekends is a nightmare when trying to fulfill normal life responsibilities.

Phase 2 was the most challenging (mentally) I have attended in my career. If someone is in a position to complete course work in their civilian of AGR position it might not be as bad, but a great deal of off time from my civilian employer was spent doing work for this class. I would prefer if there was a two week alternative for Phase 2. Our active duty counter parts get to attend school full time, and are compensated for it. We as Reservists have to do a great deal of work without compensation.

Some ADL students had similar comments about the need to work on the course on discretionary time:

I appreciate making this available at your own pace with multiple completion options, but an active duty soldier takes a time out from his career to complete ILE. A National Guard Soldier does this in ADDITION to his M-day and civilian jobs in an unpaid status for the most part. The Army has to address this issue.

Course material is interesting and deserves more attention than can be allowed through distance learning. The Phase II course requirements, which require a significant amount of time, are difficult to complete when working a 50-60 hour work week and spending time with family.

Several students in TASS and ADL commented on the importance of peer interaction and/or suggested mechanisms for collaboration:

As difficult as the course schedule was competing with work and family obligations, I think the interactive environment is essential for the subject matter discussed. I truly got a more in-depth understanding of the material from my peers in the class. (TASS)

My peers were truly the best part of the experience. They were able to discuss many of the subjects with on-site experience and it really gave me a better learning experience. (TASS)

I strongly encourage all students to attend drill weekends versus ADL. The interaction with the instructors is critical to the success of ILE. Having face-to-face interaction really added a certain learning dimension that could not be recreated with ADL online courses. All in all this is a great course. (TASS)

Some form of open discussion needs to be incorporated into the course. Further, a way to interact with the instructor of the course would be helpful. (ADL)

There never seemed to be an "instructor" to talk to about expectations or clarifications about assignments. I very much felt "on my own" doing this coursework and the military is anything but a "one soldier profession." (ADL)

Collaborate tools would be nice to discuss with other distance learning students. One aspect of the adult learning model missing in this ADL system is the ability to interact with other students. Resident students clearly learn from each other while at the school house. A weekly or monthly online session (optional) would allow ADL students to bounce ideas and questions off each other during the entire course. (ADL)

I was drinking from the fire hose during most of the lesson blocks. ...Some material was difficult to understand without having someone whom I could ask for advice. Offering some sort of monthly teleconference or a 5-min discussion could've alleviated hours of headache and running around. Heck, even the being able to call into a class session that being performed on a monthly basis would be invaluable. (ADL)

A number of TASS students also commented on the sequence in which instructors presented topics or scheduled activities. Some of these responses include:

To improve the course, I would attempt to cover all major blocks of instruction in sequence. ... all C, L, H, etc. Very confusing to go back and forth. (TASS)

Develop the course blocks to run from start to end, i.e., F101, F102, F103, F104, F105, F106, F107, F108, instead of separating them out throughout the duration of the course, i.e., F101, F102, L105, C401, H106, etc. ... I feel I would gain more out of it focusing on one topic at a time. (TASS)

Personally, I think the training schedule should not bounce around as much. Fix the blocks of instruction to conduct all the History, then all the Force Management, etc. ... And, by the time the ADL wrap around for the H100s came - the ADL had been completed months before and the information was not fresh in the minds of the students. This example was prevalent in other blocks as well. (TASS)

Make the due dates for the ADL's coincide with the wrap around discussions. (TASS)

Finally, there were a number of comments about **accessibility to Blackboard:**

We were not able to access Blackboard in the classroom, which limited our ability to enhance the experience in real time. I had difficulty accessing blackboard, until I bought my own computer, and did OK from that point on. (TASS)

Some students were locked out of Blackboard. For obvious reasons this made learning a challenge. (TASS)

Have some technical difficulty until I became familiar with the technology of Blackboard. (ADL)

The only concern is technological, the Blackboard does not support the Apple Mac computers for the submission of the assignments. (ADL)

In summary, responses to open-ended questions can be used to explore survey responses in more depth and to identify suggestions for course improvements. Responses can identify ways in which the curriculum is not being implemented as designed (e.g., if instructors are teaching lessons out of sequence) or cases in which students have an incomplete understanding about the course (e.g., responses suggested that students were not aware of help desk support). Common themes in students' comments, such as workload and course structure, can also be used to construct close-ended questions in future evaluations, which can be analyzed much more efficiently than responses to open-ended questions.

Chapter Conclusion

Responses to close-ended survey questions show that students in all venues gave favorable ratings to most aspects of the course. However, these ratings may be subject to biases and other factors that make it difficult to draw meaningful conclusions about differences among venues. In addition, the high ratings in combination with a lack of variation in responses yielded data with limited diagnostic value.

Nevertheless, some measures, particularly in combination with responses to the open-ended questions, do point to areas in which improvements in the Common Core, as well as improvements in its evaluation, may be beneficial. For example, many issues revolve around a lack of feedback from the instructor or a lack of interaction more generally. Steps can be taken to improve in those areas, and questions about feedback and interaction could be added to surveys to better monitor the effects of interventions. A complete list of recommendations is discussed in the final chapter of this report.

4. GRADES ON STUDENT ASSESSMENTS AND FACULTY GRADING PRACTICES

In this chapter, we report results of our analysis of differences among venues in average grades for assignments that were common across venues. We also present results of a quasi-experimental study examining the consistency of grading among faculty in the Common Core. Accurate grades are important to motivate students' efforts and to provide feedback about their strengths and needs for improvement; conversely, inaccurate grades or inconsistent practices may negatively affect student morale. Reliable grades can also allow course developers to identify blocks of instruction or lessons for which low student outcomes indicate that improvement may be warranted. Accurate and reliable grades are also important to reward outstanding student performance. In the resident and satellite classes, CGSS distinguishes the top 20 percent of students in each staff group as determined by grade point average (GPA) and team leader review. These students earn a designation of "Exceeds Standards" on their Academic Efficiency Report (AER), which is part of their official officer record. CGSS is considering extending this program to TASS and ADL venues as well. Thus, grades need to discriminate accurately among levels of performance.

Overview of Results

The analysis presented in this chapter will show that average grades were generally high (ranging from 88 to 92 out of 100) for most assignments in all venues. High averages, coupled with limited variation in grades, suggest grade inflation is occurring. However, even if we assume that the grades were valid, the results may be indicative of performance, but they do not reflect learning. Without information about students' levels of knowledge and skills at the outset of the course or use of a control group, we cannot evaluate the degree to which the course improved the students' abilities to perform learning goals and objectives and the extent to which venue influenced possible improvements.

Although there were statistically significant differences in grades across venues, differences were not practically significant (i.e., the differences were so small that they were not meaningful), and, with the exception of age, there were no systematic associations of grades and any of the individual-level characteristics that were available for analysis. Older students earned lower grades on all but two of the assignments assessed. Significant associations of demographic characteristics, such as age with grades, coupled with differences in the distribution of individual-level characteristics across venues, underscore the difficulty in isolating the effects of the venue and the need to control for differences in the characteristics of students.

In addition, in order to gauge student performance and conduct meaningful comparisons of performance across or within venues, faculty must be using the same standards and grading practices within and among venues. In the second part of this chapter, we present the results from our study of the consistency of grading among faculty in the Common Core. This study found that faculty members tended to be internally consistent in that there was agreement (positive correlations) in their specific ratings and overall grades. However, agreement with a standard and reliability across graders was generally quite low. We note, however, that this study has a number of limitations; of greatest concern was the extremely low response rate, coupled with the fact that most participants were resident instructors. Thus, findings may not be generalizable to the population of faculty for the Common Core, but the low levels of reliability that we found point to the need for further investigation of grading criteria and processes.

Average Grades by Venue

Analysis and Results

Figure 4.1 shows average grades on 11 assignments or exams common to all three venues. Most of these assignments consist of exams, papers, and planning products. Instructors use a rubric to grade each assignment, which is described in more detail later in this chapter. We used ANOVA to analyze differences in venues on overall grades, which consisted of scores on a 0- to 100-point scale. Analyses were based on 1,042 students in the resident course, and a range of 209 to 603 students in ADL and 843 to 1,164 students in TASS. The number of students in ADL and TASS varied because of rolling admissions (in ADL) and because some students switched between TASS and ADL venues during the course.

Average grades were generally high, ranging from 88 to 92 for most assignments in all venues. Standard deviations were small, ranging from 6 to 7 for most assessments, indicating limited variation in grades. These patterns suggest grade inflation, i.e., leniency in grading. Thus, assessments may not reflect whether students mastered the course content, and these "ceiling effects" limit the ability to discriminate among levels of performance or to observe associations with other variables.

Figure 4.1. Average Grades by Venue

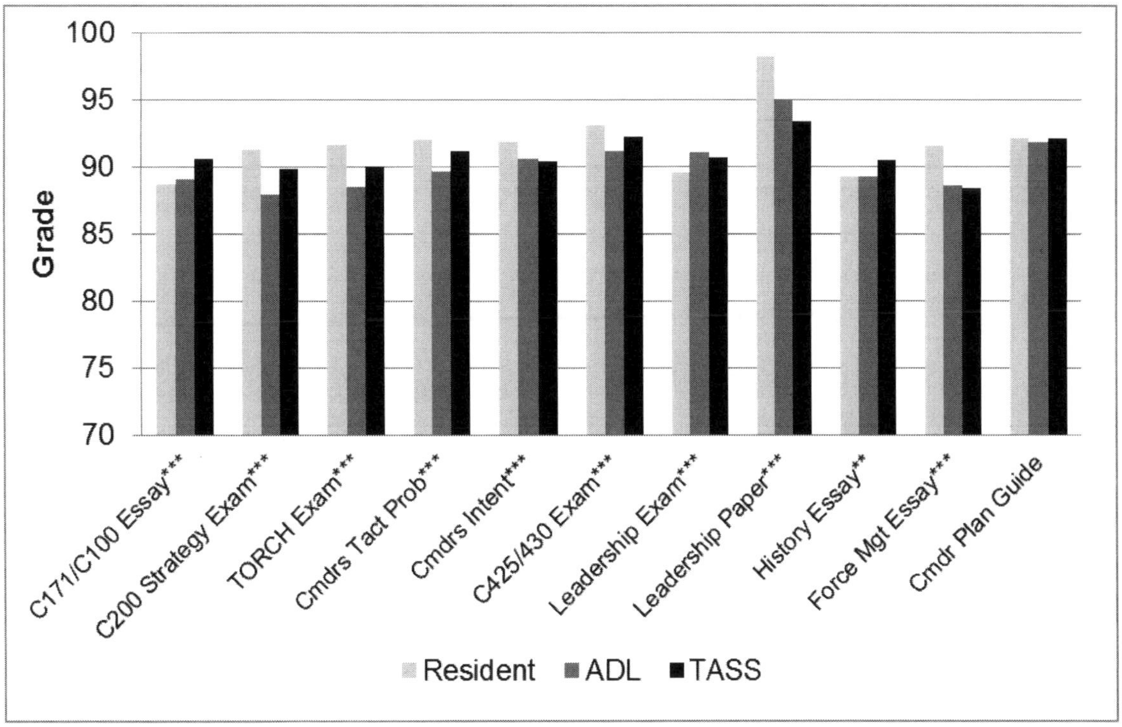

***p < 0.001

With the exception of the Commanders' Planning Guidance, differences in grades across venues were statistically significant.[43] Effect sizes, however, were small, with most ranging from 0.01 to 0.03. Venue differences were greater for the Leadership exam, with a medium effect size of 0.07. Grades on this assignment were quite high in all venues, but particularly so for resident students. Thus, there is limited practical significance of differences among venues.

In addition, the effects of venue were reduced for four assignments (the C200 exam, TORCH exam, Commander's Tactical Problem, and Commander's Intent) when accounting for individual-level characteristics. We included variables that were available for students all venues, which included age, rank, gender, and component.[44] Table 4.1 shows descriptive statistics of demographic characteristics by venue. There were statistically significant differences in these characteristics across venues, with especially large effects for component.

---

[43] Sample size influences statistical significance; significance of the differences in venues may be due to the large number of observations in each venue.

[44] Availability of other individual-level variables varied by venue; for example, the resident data include college or university, discipline, highest degree, and marital status; TASS and ADL included branch, date of commission, and time in rank.

Table 4.1. Demographic Characteristics by Venue

Characteristic	Venue			Venue differences
	Resident	**ADL**	**TASS**	
Average age (SD)	38.5 (3.81)	40.5(5.67)	41.2(5.26)	***
Rank				***
Chief WO (3-5)	< 1%	0	0	
CPT	< 1%	23%	21%	
MAJ	93%	76%	78%	
LTC	3%	0	0	
Civilian	2%	0	0	
Not available		< 1%	< 1%	
Male	90.1%	83%	82%	***
Component[a]				***
Regular Army	72%	16%	5%	
ARNG	3%	29%	36%	
Army Reserve	4%	0	< 1%	
Other service	13%	2%	0	
International Military	6%	< 1%	0	
Army Civilian	0	< 1%	< 1%	
Not available	2%	52%	59%	

[a] Percentages may not sum to 100 percent because of rounding.
***$p < 0.001$

For the analyses of demographic characteristics, we consolidated some components and ranks because of the small number of students in some categories. Components in the analysis included AC, RC, and "other" (which included other services and international military students). Because not all variables were included in each survey, information about component was not available for more than 1,800 students. These students, primarily from TASS and ADL, were excluded from the analysis (see last row of Table 4.1). Ranks included Warrant Officer, Captain, Major, Lieutenant Colonel, and other (civilians).

Table 4.2 summarizes the results of comparisons of grades across venues when including these individual-level variables. The symbols indicate variables that were significantly associated with grades. For example, in the first row of the table, the symbols indicate that there were significant associations of grades on the C171/C100 essay with venue, component, and age, but not with rank and gender.

The most consistent result showed a negative association of age and grades, with older students earning lower grades on all but two assignments. The effect size for this result was small to medium, and the negative association of grades and age was stronger among resident students than among ADL and TASS students. For the five assignments or exams for which component had an effect, in most cases, "other" military and civilians tended to get higher grades than did AC officers, who in turn had higher grades than officers in the RC, although these effects were small. For the assignments or tests shown in bold and italics, the effect of venue dropped (but remained statistically significant) after inclusion of the individual-level variables.

Table 4.2. Association of Venue and Demographic Characteristics with Grades

Assignment or Exam	Venue	Component	Rank	Gender	Age
C171/C100 essay	•	•			•
C200 Strategy exam	•	•			•
TORCH exam	•	•			•
Cmdrs Tact Prob	•				•
Cmdrs Intent	•			•	•
C425/430 exam	•				
Leadership exam	•				•
Leadership paper	•	•			
History essay	•	•			•
Force Mgt essay	•				•
Cmdr Plan Guide				•	•

NOTE: For the assignments or tests shown in bold and italics, the effect of venue dropped (but remained statistically significant) after inclusion of the individual-level variables.

While inclusion of demographic characteristics did not eliminate venue differences, significant associations of demographic characteristics and grades, coupled with differences in the distribution of characteristics across venues, underscores the difficulty in interpreting main effects of venue and the need to control for differences in characteristics of students – particularly characteristics that are associated with academic performance. In particular, measures of general cognitive ability are strong predictors of academic performance. College degree and discipline were collected only for students in the resident course but were not provided in a standardized format.[45] Students in the resident course take the Nelson-Denny reading comprehension test, but their scores were not available for these analyses, and this test is not administered to students in the other venues.

---

[45] This was self-reported data, and it appears that students entered their responses in a free-text field rather than selecting from a list of standard responses such as "bachelor's," "master's," etc. The responses were highly variable and difficult to interpret; there were over 25 categories of what appear to be bachelor's degrees, over 40 categories of apparent master's degrees, and a number of responses that were ambiguous (e.g., "Engineering," "Sci," "SH," and "Yes").

Motivational disposition or orientation (or learning goal orientation) is another individual characteristic that is associated with performance in education and training (e.g., Fisher and Ford, 1998; Klein, Noe, and Wang, 2006; Mesmer-Magnus and Viswesvaran, 2007). Individuals who have a mastery orientation emphasize learning for self-improvement, skill development, and long-term competence, whereas individuals with a performance orientation are focused on doing well on outcomes (e.g., on tests), typically to gain positive evaluations or avoid negative evaluations (e.g., Dweck, 1986). Motivation to learn refers to the desire to learn the content of a training program or course, which influences how individuals engage and persist in learning activities (Noe, 1986). Learning goal orientation and motivation to learn may be especially important in web-based and blended-learning environments, where students have substantial responsibility for and control over when and how learning takes place (Klein, Noe, and Wang, 2006). Therefore, collecting these sorts of individual-level variables could help determine if there are meaningful effects of venue on performance in the Common Core.[46]

Limitations

A consideration regarding these analyses is that they do not speak to the validity of the grades in terms of measuring Common Core learning goals and TLO achievement. **In addition, even if we assume that the grades were valid, the results may be indicative of performance, but they do not reflect learning.** That is, without information about students' levels of knowledge and skills at the outset of the course or use of a control group, it is not possible to evaluate the degree to which the course improved the students' abilities and the extent to which venue influenced possible improvements. Moreover, given differences in student populations across venues, it is very possible that there was variation in initial knowledge and skills among venues that affected grades in the course. Reliable data about individual-level variables that are strongly associated with academic performance, such as general cognitive ability and learning goal orientation, are needed to control for student factors to better understand effects of venue.

Section Conclusion

In sum, grades were generally high on assessments, and differences among venues had little practical significance. With the exception of age, there were no systematic associations of grades and individual-level characteristics. This finding is in contrast to results of other studies that have generally found positive associations among age and outcomes in adult education (e.g., Hoskins, Newstead, and Dennis, 1997; Koch, 2006). The reasons for the negative association for Common Core students are not entirely clear, although it appears to be related to component. That is, there were systematic differences in age by component, with the oldest students in the

---

[46] While these characteristics are often viewed as disposition traits, there also is evidence that they are domain specific and can be induced (e.g., Klein, Noe, and Wang, 2006; Mesmer-Magnus and Viswesvaran, 2007). Given the focus on critical thinking skills in CGSOC, it may be worthwhile to examine mastery orientation before and after the course.

RC (average age = 40.12), the youngest students in the "Other" category (average age = 37.5), and AC students in the middle (average age = 39). There were corresponding differences in grades for several assignments, such that students in the "Other" component received the highest grades, followed by AC and then RC students. It is not clear, however, why the "Other" students earned higher grades.[47] One hypothesis is that older students (e.g., over 40) may be close to retirement and therefore are less concerned about earning high grades, whereas younger officers are competing for commands and therefore are motivated to earn a designation of "Exceeds Standards" on their AER. Yet another hypothesis is that older students have been away from an academic environment longer and were less accustomed to the coursework.

In addition, in order to gauge student performance and conduct meaningful comparisons of performance across venues, faculty must be using the same standards and grading practices within and across venues. It is possible that differences in faculty characteristics across venues (e.g., in terms of professional development opportunities or teaching experience) and differences in student characteristics influence grades. For example, there may be variation in the quality of students' answers associated with systematic differences in their experience relevant to the Common Core or in their personal circumstances (e.g., time commitments) across venues, or faculty may adjust their expectations based on students' backgrounds. Because instructor characteristics and student characteristics vary systematically with venue, direct comparisons of grades across venues may be masking these effects.

Evaluation of Faculty Reliability in Grading

Some initial evidence from the ADL course indicates that faculty are not always consistent in grading. Assignments from 44 ADL students across a variety of blocks were inadvertently graded by two different graders. The correlation between the two sets of grades was not statistically significant, with a small-to-medium effect size ($r = 0.20$). There were two cases in which assigned grades were highly discrepant; removing these cases resulted in a medium-to-large and statistically significant association between grades ($r = 0.45$, $p < 0.01$).

These results are mixed and are limited to ADL faculty. To explore reliability in grading more systematically, we conducted a quasi-experimental study in which course instructors in resident and TASS venues and adjunct faculty in ADL (all are subsequently referred to as "faculty") were asked to grade a sample of student answers to one of four exams: TORCH, Tactics, History, and Leadership. Holding student answers constant enabled us to control for

---

[47] One possible explanation is that faculty members take the student's background into account when grading papers and may have lower expectations for students from outside the Army, resulting in higher grades for these students. This hypothesis is suggested by findings from the study of grader reliability, presented later in this chapter.

potential differences in the quality of answers across venues.[48] A detailed description of the method and results follows.

Method

Sampling. CGSS provided RAND with contact information for faculty in each venue, stratified by the types of exams that each faculty member was qualified to grade (i.e., in resident and ADL venues, faculty grade exams in their areas of specialty; in TASS, graders are generalists and grade all exams). We randomly selected up to 50 faculty per exam topic in each venue where possible; if there were fewer than 50 faculty, we selected all eligible faculty. Four-hundred and fifty-two faculty members were invited to participate. The number of faculty recruited by venue and exam type is shown in Table 4.3.

Table 4.3. Number of Faculty Sampled by Venue and Exam

Exam	Venue		
	Resident	ADL	TASS
TORCH	50	24	50
Tactics	50	22	50
History	30	24	50
Leadership	28	24	50

Recruiting. CGSS staff sent a message informing leaders in each venue about the study and asked their assistance to promote the study to the faculty. Leaders were asked to send a prepared message to faculty regarding participation. RAND followed up with an email invitation to participate and several reminder messages.

Materials. CGSS staff selected four exemplar answers for each exam; one "A" level paper, two "B" level papers, and one "C" level paper. ADL students' answers were used because they were submitted and stored electronically, whereas copies of prior answers from resident and TASS venues had not been retained. Information about student identity and venue was removed from the answers.

Each faculty member received a packet consisting of an instruction sheet, an information sheet that served as the informed consent protocol, four student answers in one of four possible orders, 1009w grading forms, the relevant grading rubric provided by CGSS, and a survey with questions about participant demographic characteristics, experience, comments about the study, and comments about the grading process more generally. Rubrics provided criteria for grading the assignments. 1009w forms are used to give feedback to students. For each assignment,

---

[48] We also attempted to control for potential differences among faculty by collecting information about their backgrounds; however, we were not able to use these data because of the small number of study participants.

faculty are asked to provide an overall grade; indicate the cognitive level attained, which included evaluation, synthesis, analysis, application, comprehension, and knowledge (ranging from high to low); and give ratings ranging from 1 to 5 on "substance details" of the student's work including content, analysis/problem solving/conclusion, organization, style, and correctness.

Procedures. RAND sent hard copies of the packets to CGSS, who distributed them to faculty in resident and TASS venues. RAND sent electronic versions consisting of Microsoft Word documents to faculty in ADL. Participants were asked to grade the answers using the methods that they typically use to grade tests and assignments. They were informed that their participation was voluntary and anonymous. We provided self-addressed stamped envelopes for resident and TASS faculty to return their completed packets. ADL faculty were asked to upload the graded materials anonymously to a website created using SelectSurvey, which is a commercially available tool developed by ClassApps. The file upload system was hosted on a secure RAND server.

Analyses. Analyses of the data included:

1. Intra-rater reliability, or the association of participants' ratings of substance details and cognitive level attained with overall grade on the 1009w form
2. The correlation of overall grades with original exemplar grades
3. Inter-rater reliability, or agreement among different faculty on grades of the same assignments.

As a result of the low response rates, as described below, we analyzed data across all faculty rather than comparing levels of consistency among venues. We present results by exam topic where possible.[49]

There were a number of inconsistencies in how faculty provided overall grades (i.e., numeric versus letter grades, even within the same grader). Some participants used scores on a 100-point scale, some used an 80-point scale, and others used letter grades. We normalized numerical grades by creating percentages, and we dropped alphabetic grades.[50] Some participants did not give substance details ratings; these cases were eliminated from analysis (1) above. In addition, some participants did not grade all four assignments in their packets. As a result, samples sizes differ for the analyses.

---

[49] We had planned to analyze the association of grades with participant characteristics. However, in addition to the small sample size overall, many participants did not provide a grade for all four assignments, which was required for this analysis, or they did not complete the survey. In addition, there were very few participants in some categories of the demographic variables (for example, few participants had less than 20 years of military experience). Thus, we cannot draw firm conclusions about the association of participant characteristics and grades.

[50] Unless noted, converting letter grades to numbers, e.g., A = 95, B = 85, etc., has minimal impact on the results.

Results

Participants. Table 4.4 shows the number of participants per venue and exam. Forty-nine faculty members participated in the study, representing an overall response rate of 11 percent. Response rates within venue were 24 percent in resident, 6.4 percent in ADL, and 2.5 percent in TASS. The majority of responses were submitted for the Tactics and TORCH exams by resident instructors.

Table 4.4. Number of Participants by Venue and Exam

Exam	Venue		
	Resident	**ADL**	**TASS**
TORCH	11	0	1
Tactics	20	2	1
History	6	2	4
Leadership	1	1	9

Ninety percent of participants reported spending over one hour on the task; 36 percent reported spending over two hours. Appendix F shows participant characteristics. In general, the participants appeared to be moderately to very qualified in terms of military and teaching experience.

Intra-rater reliability. Fifty-three out of a possible 196 assignments (i.e., four assignments for each of 49 participants) included ratings of substance details and cognitive level attained as well as a numeric overall grade. Bivariate correlations between overall grade and the specific ratings showed that participants were internally consistent. That is, the overall grades that participants gave were positively associated with their specific ratings, as shown in Table 4.5.

Table 4.5. Correlation of Overall Grades with Ratings of Cognitive Level and Substance Details

Rating	Correlation with Overall Grade
Cognitive level attained	0.57***
Content	0.80***
Analysis/problem-solving/conclusions	0.74***
Organization	0.74***
Style	0.51***
Correctness	0.34***

***$p < 0.001$.

58

In addition, multiple regression showed that the set of specific ratings accounted for 74 percent of the variance in overall grades.[51] Content, analysis/problem-solving/conclusions, organization, and cognitive level were significantly associated with overall grade, whereas style and correctness were not. Thus, specific ratings concerned with higher-level thinking skills were most strongly associated with overall grade. Note that these findings do not indicate whether participants' grades were accurate; merely that they were internally consistent in grading. It is notable, however, that they were internally consistent despite the lack of any explicit link between the specific ratings and overall grade in the 1009w form (e.g., graders are not told to use ratings of cognitive level attained and/or substance details to determine the overall grade).

Association of overall grades with original exemplar grades. Table 4.6 shows the association of grades for each assignment with the original exemplar grades. The overall correlation between grades given in the study and exemplar grades was -0.08 and was not statistically different from zero (*ns*). Likewise, correlations for each assignment and its exemplar were not statistically significant.[52] Results were similar for resident faculty alone, with an overall correlation of -0.15, *ns*. **Thus, there was no association of participants' evaluations with the original exemplar grades.**

Table 4.6. Average Grades by Exemplar

Assignment	Exemplar		
	"A"	"B"	"C"
TORCH	72.6	76.5	77.7
Tactics	72.4	82.6	78.4
Leadership	86.0	77.0	86.0[a]
History	83.9	82.6	78.6
Overall	76.0	80.7	78.6

[a]Small sample size.

Figures 4.2 and 4.3 show the dispersion of grades for each exemplar for the Tactics and TORCH exams, respectively. Each dot in the figure represents one graded assignment. The top, middle, and bottom bands display grades given for the "A," "B," and "C" exemplars, respectively, and the darker shaded area within each band shows the approximate region of the graph in which grades were expected to cluster.

---

[51] $R^2 = 0.74$, $F(6,46) = 22.12$, $p < 0.001$.

[52] For the TORCH exam, $r = -0.12$; for the Tactics exam, $r = -0.18$; for the History exam, $r = 0.19$. This analysis was not reported for the Leadership exam because of the extremely small number of responses. The result for the History exam improves somewhat when including letter grades that were converted to numbers, $r = 0.27$, $p < 0.10$.

The figures show the wide distribution of grades given, regardless of the assignments' original grades. A similar distribution was found for the History exam. Data for the Leadership exam are not presented because of the small sample size.

Figure 4.2. Distribution of Grades by Exemplar for the Tactics Exam

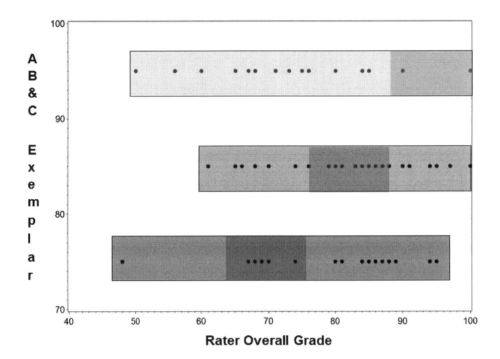

Figure 4.3. Distribution of Grades by Exemplar for the TORCH Exam

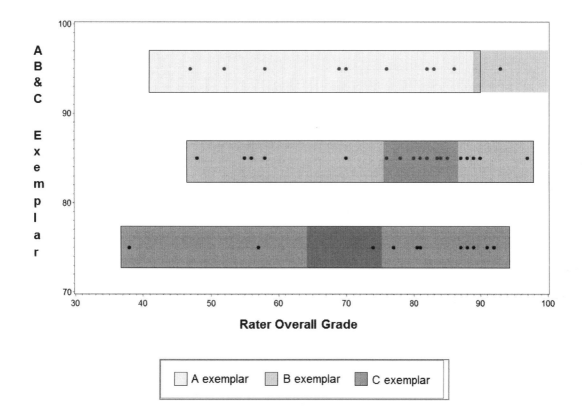

Inter-rater reliability. Inter-rater reliability was assessed for the History, TORCH, and Tactics exams across all four essays using intraclass correlations (ICCs) that assume the raters are a random sample of the population of raters (ICC[2,1] and ICC[2,k]) (Shrout and Fleiss, 1979).

Results indicate low inter-rater reliability for each exam. The reliability of any single rater was $r = -0.01$ ($p = 0.469$) for History, $r = 0.01$ ($p = 0.165$) for TORCH, and $r = 0.15$ ($p < 0.001$) for Tactics. If one considers the average reliability for all the raters for each exam, the reliability was $r = -0.10$ for History, $r = 0.01$ for TORCH, and $r = 0.77$ for Tactics (for p-values, see above). These results indicate little or no relationship between scores given to each essay across raters for the History and TORCH exams. The significant ICC for Tactics indicates some degree of rater agreement in their scores. However, given the number of raters in the study, the correlation of 0.77 is considered weak.

Grades and individual differences. Analysis shows that there were individual differences in grading across graders (although the small number of responses does not allow us to analyze specific types of individual differences, such as demographics, with grades).[53] Figure 4.4

---

[53] $F(43,116) = 4.85$, $p < 0.001$, $\eta^2 = 0.64$.

displays the average grade (denoted by the circles) and standard deviation (denoted by the bars) for each participant that graded all four assignments. The results indicate that approximately two-thirds of the participants gave scores of 80 or above, but there were several participants who gave extremely low grades, and there was substantial variation among participants. For some participants, such as Graders 8 and 35, the range of grades given was very narrow, indicating that they did not discriminate among the exemplars. For others, such as Graders 13 and 28, the range was substantial (although it did not necessarily correspond to the exemplar grades).

Figure 4.4. Average Grade by Participant

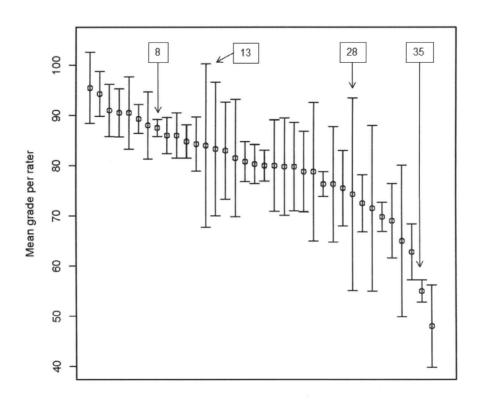

Rater

Qualitative findings. We reviewed written comments that participants provided to students on the papers and on the 1009w forms.

In general, resident and TASS faculty members were very thorough and detailed. Some faculty even offered to meet with students to elaborate on their written feedback. Comments were often very frank (sometimes severely so) when work did not meet standards. However, the thoroughness of the written feedback meant that it was sometimes difficult to wade through all the comments, and some comments were illegible. In ADL, some faculty members used "Track changes" to provide comments directly on student papers, and all participants wrote comments on the 1009w grading form. **Most of the ADL faculty, however, focused on correctness (grammar) and style rather than on substance. With few exceptions, their substantive comments were minimal and lacked specificity.** It is important to note, however, that few ADL faculty participated, so we cannot generalize from these observations to the population of ADL faculty as a whole.

Participants also had some comments about grading practices, many of which concerned subjectivity of grading and quality of rubrics. Some participants remarked that there is a lack of attention paid to how to grade exams except within teaching teams or that grading is not addressed sufficiently in FDP.[54] On the other hand, one participant felt that it is counterproductive to "micromanage" grading because it is inherently subjective and because the context promotes widespread grade inflation. The participant emphasized that many instructors seek to improve officers' knowledge and skills during CGSOC but feel that it is not their responsibility to remove officers who are not qualified to be in their positions (which can occur if a student receives a "C" in two lessons).

Some participants reported that the rubrics were inadequate, e.g.,

> Rubrics need to be more encompassing. They need to list the mini requirement and provide "other alternatives." Seldom is the [SIC] one single right answer so we (especially new instructors) need to know or see the left and right limits of possible answers.

> The guidance that is available for the TORCH exam is ... excellent and detailed. I can be assured that I will grade each person's paper the same. This has not been true of some of the other assignments.

> The grading guidance provided was very flawed. I grade IAW [in accordance with] current guidance since this was in fact terrible guidance.

> Your [SIC] rubrics for this exam were poor. They did not properly explain what you were looking for and what the student was expected to produce.

> If we are going to use rubrics, the point totals assessed should equal the grade. Simply checking a box from 1 to 5 (low to high) does nothing to calibrate grades or promote consistency. Grading is arbitrary unless a standard is provided with point equivalents.

---

[54] These comments are surprising in light of the FDP curriculum, which addresses grading practices. In addition, CGSS provides the lesson author contact information and school contact information in case instructors have questions about lesson requirements.

Another participant recommended providing rating scales with more than five points. He or she remarked that it is a rare student who answers a question "perfectly" and deserves a 5 for each part of the exam, but giving a 4 on a 5-point scale results in an overall score of 80 percent, or a "B," even for A-level answers.

Several participants' comments about their typical grading approach were instructive regarding internal consistency. For example, some remarks suggest that faculty weighted the substance details to systematically determine overall grade, e.g., "Style and grammar account for 10% of the overall grade." Two participants noted that by not knowing which students wrote the answers, the study was not representative of actual practice because they take the students' background (e.g., career field or native language) into account when grading. It is also interesting that one of the students perceived that peers were held to different standards, as reported in response to an open-ended survey question. The student commented, "We had one JAG officer in the class that wrote for a congressman and he had multiple redos which made me think that they graded him harder."

Limitations

This study has a number of limitations. An issue specific to the TORCH exam was that at the time the study was fielded, faculty had just started grading for the new academic year. Anecdotal evidence indicated that some participants may have used the new rubric (rather than the rubric provided in the packets) to grade answers from a prior academic year. This issue could account, in part, for low inter-rater reliability and poor correspondence with the exemplar grades for the TORCH exam.

More important, however, is that additional investigation is needed to determine if findings generalize to the population of faculty for the Common Core. The response rate to the study was quite low (especially outside the resident venue), likely because participation was voluntary and the task was labor intensive. The small number of responses may not provide sufficient statistical power to detect "true" effects, and the results are most likely subject to selection bias in that participants may differ systematically from non-participants. In addition, because this was an experiment, the manner in which participants graded students' answers may not be representative of their typical grading practices. Some faculty may have felt compelled to grade more rigorously than usual because they knew this was an evaluation; others may have exerted less effort because their participation was anonymous; and comments from the participants cited above indicate that other aspects of the study did not replicate the ways that they typically grade. At the same time, one might expect that the faculty who did participate were particularly conscientious. Moreover, most participants had extensive experience and they reported spending a substantial amount of time grading the assignments for the study. Thus, the results could indicate a best case scenario in terms of grading consistency.

An additional issue was the participants varied in how they used the 1009w form in terms of providing alphabetic or numeric grades and in ratings of substance details. This was a limitation of the study in that it resulted in incomplete data for the analyses. However, this is also a substantive finding in that it shows a lack of consistency in how feedback is being provided to students. Incomplete or inconsistent data also preclude the use of specific ratings to calculate overall grade in a systematic way.

Section Conclusion

In sum, faculty members tended to be internally consistent in that there was agreement in their specific ratings and overall grades. However, reliability across raters was generally quite low. For the History and TORCH exams, there was little or no relationship among scores across raters who evaluated the same student assignments. In the concluding chapter, we recommend further investigation of grading practices in the three venues. If these results generalize to the faculty more broadly, then remedial action, such as professional development, would be needed to ensure that faculty have a common understanding about grading standards.

5. SUMMARY, CONCLUSIONS, AND THE WAY AHEAD

In this chapter, we summarize the overarching conclusions from our study, offer suggestions for improvement in the Common Core, and provide directions for future evaluation.

Conclusions

In general, favorable responses in the surveys suggest that students feel that they are learning the material in the Common Core and are satisfied with most aspects of instructional delivery. In addition, average grades on assessments were high across venues.

Analysis of students' attitudes about cognitive learning and grades on assignments and tests show no meaningful differences in outcomes among the three venues. Because ADL provides a far less costly method of instruction than the resident or TASS venues, these outcomes might lead one to conclude that ADL should be used exclusively to teach the Common Core.

However, these results should not be interpreted to mean that the venues are equally effective or that differences do not exist. For many reasons, we cannot draw conclusions about levels of learning (despite large sample sizes) or about differences among venues in students' attitudes.

- There are a variety of fundamental differences or confounds among venues in factors that may influence learning and attitudes, including the different populations attending the course and student levels of knowledge prior to enrolling. In addition, basic design differences in the course across venues, such as course length, instructor qualifications, and the degree of instructor-student and peer interaction, mean that we cannot identify how particular aspects of the course influenced students' reactions or student performance.
- Although faculty who participated in this research were internally consistent in grading, they generally were not consistent with peers, which means that comparing venues in terms of student grades may not be meaningful. In addition, one cannot draw conclusions about learning from course grades because of an absence of data about pre-course knowledge and aptitude in combination with some of the other issues mentioned above. Student self-assessments of learning, while generally positive, are also not a replacement for objective measures of cognitive learning (Sitzmann et al., 2010b).
- Analyses of responses to the student surveys suggest that there were systematic response biases, particularly careless responding.

Moreover, we would not expect the venues to have equivalent outcomes. Although the learning goals are the same in all venues of the Common Core, the venues are designed to support very different student environments and needs. Our analysis of the characteristics of the venues showed substantial differences in factors such as instructor qualifications and degree of instructor-student and peer interaction. These differences are meaningful enough that they would logically lead to expectations that learning outcomes and student reactions and attitudes will differ across venues. This conclusion is substantiated by other research that asked Common Core graduates from different venues to compare their experience in the Common Core to the follow on AOC course taught via distributed blended learning (see Straus et al., 2013).

Suggestions for Improvement

Given that the Army will likely have an ongoing need to provide the Common Core in different venues, future evaluation should focus on whether the best possible outcomes within venues, rather than equivalent outcomes across venues, are achieved. Although there is often a tendency to want to compare distributed learning and resident instruction, the data requirements to conduct robust comparisons of venues are very demanding and may be unattainable. An effective comparison requires collecting a comprehensive set of explanatory variables that can control for inherent differences in venues and can be used to rule out alternative explanations. Furthermore, given systematic differences among venues (e.g., the resident venue is mostly AC students, whereas TASS and ADL are largely RC students; faculty in each venue have different qualifications), it is likely infeasible to control for all of the important differences. The recommendation to focus on improvement within each venue is consistent with prior conclusions in analyses of delivery venues for Army training (Straus et al., 2006).

With this premise in mind, we present suggestions to address the following questions:

- What improvements can be made to the Common Core within each venue?
- How can current methods of evaluation be improved?
- What other methods of evaluation and metrics are appropriate for the Common Core?
- What organizational supports are needed to improve evaluation efforts?

Improving the Common Core

Table 5.1 summarizes recommendations for improving students' experiences in the Common Core. We discuss each in detail below.

Table 5.1. Recommendations to Improve Common Core Delivery

Goal	Strategies
1. Ensure faculty consistency in grading	• Further investigate consistency across venues • Provide professional development • Provide clearer grading standards • Solicit faculty input about grading criteria and process
2. Identify opportunities for instructor and peer interaction in ADL	• Schedule weekly office hours with instructors using online chat, web conferencing, or audio conferencing • Allow remote students to dial in to resident or TASS class discussions • Encourage interaction via online discussion boards
3. Ensure technical reliability of ADL software	• Move to a dotcom platform (in progress) • Provide training or tutorials on use of the courseware • Provide increased availability or awareness of technical support • Collect more diagnostic information about technical issues
4. Establish clear expectations for ADL	• Review content of welcome letter • Consider alternatives for orientation material, e.g., webinar or online tutorial
5. Reduce burden in TASS and ADL Phase II	• Consider alternative structures, e.g., for TASS using ADT or ADT coupled with weekend IDTs or move more lessons to ADL and use IDT sessions for discussion and review • Deliver all of Phase II material via ADL and supplement it with opportunities for remote interaction (see Goal 2 above)

The most important area to address in the Common Core is ensuring that faculty are consistent in grading. Although findings from the study of reliability in grading may be considered tentative, the exceptionally low levels of inter-rater reliability suggest the need to investigate grading practices further and to take steps, if necessary, to achieve greater consistency among faculty. While we do not advocate micromanaging the grading process, improving consistency in feedback is important because of inherent subjectivity in grading of Common Core assignments and because students, especially those in resident and ADL venues, prepare their work for numerous, different faculty who may have different styles and perspectives.

CGSS has addressed this issue, in part, by sampling graded assignments from adjunct faculty and providing them to resident instructors for re-grading; in addition, assignments that receive grades of C or lower from any faculty member (full time or adjunct) are re-graded by a second instructor. In addition, CGSS plans to increase the role of full-time faculty in grading for ADL. These changes may be sufficient to achieve consistency; however, if further investigation reveals that a lack of consistency persists among the faculty more generally, professional development may be needed to (1) address the types of comments and level of detail expected when grading student papers and completing the 1009w form and (2) provide clear standards for grades both in terms of what constitutes an "A," "B," and so forth; what constitutes the need for a "redo;" the format for assigning grades (e.g., letter or numerical grades); and whether it is acceptable to take

69

a student's background into account when grading assignments. In addition, there should be clear expectations for turnaround times on papers and exams. CGSS might also consider revising the 1009w form to allow for finer distinctions in ratings for substance details (e.g., allow graders to use fractions, such as 4.5) and to specify how the substance details should be weighted in determining overall grade (with presumably more weight on substantive and analytical issues rather than on style and correctness). We recommend soliciting input from faculty about the grading criteria and process to identify needed improvements.

Improving grading practices can also address students' concerns about feedback, which emerged primarily in answers to close-ended questions in ADL surveys and open-ended remarks from TASS students. These responses indicate that many students would like to receive feedback that is more specific (particularly in ADL), and more timely (in ADL and TASS). **Aside from ratings of feedback, however, the survey responses point to only a small number of areas for improvement.**

A second suggestion, which is related to concerns about feedback, is to provide ADL students with opportunities for instructor and peer interaction by using distributed blended learning strategies. This suggestion is based on comments from ADL students, who expressed a desire for interaction, and from TASS students, who described the value of interaction in supporting their learning. We expect that interaction with peers and instructors is especially important for the Common Core, which involves development and application of analytical and critical thinking skills (compared to courses in which the material is more concrete and answers or solutions are demonstrably correct). Blended learning can improve pedagogy by supporting a wide range of learning methods, including learner-centered strategies and opportunities to connect with representatives from outside organizations, such as guest speakers (Theroux and Kilbane, 2005). Providing ADL students with opportunities for instructor and peer interaction is also consistent with findings from a previous RAND study of student reactions to Army DL (Straus et al., 2011) as well as with the research literature on web-based instruction more generally (e.g., Sitzmann, Ely, and Wisher, 2008).

There are many ways to provide opportunities for interaction with instructors and peers; for example, instructors could hold weekly office hours using online chat or an audio-conference line; remote students could be allowed to dial in to resident or TASS class discussions (as suggested by one of the students); instructors and students with webcams could use video chat for one-on-one interactions; and online discussion boards could be offered as a way for students to interact with each other or to respond to instructor-initiated discussion topics.

In fact, as described in Chapter 2, CGSS already uses some of these strategies – along with other forms of technology-mediated interaction – for AOC, the follow-on course to the Common Core. AOC is completely distributed and is supported by a range of technologies for online synchronous interaction, including Blackboard's learning management system and Defense Connect Online. In short, CGSS could shift the ADL course from strict IMI to include elements of distributed blended learning, applying methods used in AOC. CGSS would need to investigate the resourcing requirements for these alternatives (e.g., for instructors), particularly given the large number of students who take the Common Core.

Third, the survey results indicate the need to address some technical issues with ADL software. As documented by Sitzmann et al. (2010a), technical difficulties can result in poorer performance and greater attrition in online courses (although we note that attrition in the Common Core is quite low, at less than 5 percent). TASS students experienced a number of technical problems, which suggests the need for training or tutorials on use of the courseware and greater availability of technical support (or increased awareness of existing resources for technical support). In fact, CGSS is moving the ADL lessons from a dotmil to a dotcom domain. CGSS staff report that operating in a dotcom has improved speed substantially and alleviated technology reliability issues.

Future evaluation efforts could collect more diagnostic information by expanding on questions about technical issues. In the current surveys, the use of "yes" and "no" response options for questions about technical problems does not indicate the degree of these problems, i.e., did the issues significantly impede progress on the course? In future surveys, "yes" responses to questions about technical difficulties could be followed by alternatives about the impact of the problem, e.g., minimal, moderate, or substantial impediment to working on the course.

Fourth, we suggest investigating reasons why some students felt unclear about what was expected of them in ADL. Currently, students receive a welcome letter from DDE that orients them to the course. They also have a counselor and help desk that are available to assist them. It may be that additional content is needed in the welcome letter or that the information could be delivered more effectively using other methods, such as a Webinar, online tutorial, or video presentation. This sort of orientation might also be helpful for students for Phase II in TASS, which relies heavily on ADL lessons.

Finally, CGSS should consider modifications to the structure of Phase II in TASS and ADL. Comments from numerous TASS students emphasized the considerable burden they face during Phase II and the negative impact of the current structure on their ability to learn the course material. ADL students had similar comments and rated Phase II as considerably more difficult than Phases I and III. Certainly both IDT and ADT training environments pose challenges for students, and many TASS students recommended making Phase II a two-week course. Given the current curriculum, this suggestion is impractical; a two-week period would provide less class time than is allotted in eight weekend sessions, which already have very long classroom hours and cover a large amount of material. However, there are variations on this theme that may better accommodate student needs and meet CGSS goals (some of which are already being offered or pilot tested by CGSS):

- For TASS, offer Phase II in a three-week ADT phase or in a two-week ADT phase coupled with three weekend IDTs. Currently, a two-week ADT version of Phase II is being tested in Europe; this pilot may provide valuable lessons regarding feasibility of this option.

- For TASS, move more of the lessons to ADL and use IDT sessions for discussion and review.
- Deliver all the Phase II material via ADL and supplement it with some of the blended learning methods discussed above. CGSS currently offers an option to complete Phase II via ADL without blended learning methods.

Each of these suggestions has pros and cons, such as cost (students would need to be paid for ADT), student preferences (many TASS students strongly preferred face-to-face instruction), and burden on students (ADL lessons would need to be completed on students' discretionary time, which is limited, and they would not necessarily be paid). However, we see the length and complexity of Phase II for both ADL and TASS students, and the long days and non-contiguous structure of Phase II TASS, as important concerns. These issues and possible mitigation strategies should be examined in more depth.

Improving Evaluation of the Common Core

Table 5.2 summarizes recommendations for improving evaluation of the Common Core.

Table 5.2. Recommendations to Improve Common Core Evaluation

Goal	Strategies
1. Acquire better diagnostic information from surveys and reduce response burden	<ul><li>To assess cognitive learning, replace current questions with pre-training and post-training measures of self-efficacy</li><li>Assess satisfaction with training in a separate, anonymous survey</li><li>Ask fewer detailed questions about each topic or ask more global questions</li><li>Sample students to complete surveys in the resident course</li><li>For satisfaction measures, use six-point response option with no neutral midpoint</li><li>Systematically analyze responses to open-ended questions</li><li>Modify survey questions over time to explore emerging issues</li><li>Use web analytics to assess time spent on surveys</li></ul>
2. Assess other outcomes	<ul><li>Conduct follow-up surveys of graduates</li><li>Conduct surveys of graduates' supervisors</li><li>Use web analytics to examine association of effort in course with performance</li></ul>

Modifications to the surveys could enhance their usefulness as part of a comprehensive program of evaluation. We recommend continuation of student surveys, assessing both reactions to the course and perceived accomplishment of course objectives. However, we propose several revisions to survey content and administration to obtain more diagnostic information and reduce response burden, and we recommend collecting other measures to evaluate the effectiveness of the Common Core.

72

First, for questions about cognitive learning, use item formats and response options that are typically used in surveys of self-efficacy. Measures of self-efficacy or self-assessments of absolute knowledge (rather than knowledge gain) are more strongly associated with cognitive learning outcomes than are measures of learner reactions or perceived knowledge gain (Sitzmann et al., 2008; Sitzmann et al., 2010b). Self-efficacy scales frequently consist of a list of tasks, and respondents are asked to rate their confidence in performing each task using a scale from 0 to 100 with 10 point increments, where 0 = "cannot do at all," 50 = "moderately can do," and 100 = "highly certain can do" (Bandura, 2006). Bandura (2006) advises against using scales with only a few response options because they are less sensitive and less reliable. Pajares, Hartley, and Valiante (2001) found that an efficacy scale with the 0-100 response format was psychometrically stronger and was a better predictor of performance than a scale with a 5-point Likert-type scale.

Thus, self-efficacy for some of the Planning topics in C600 might be presented as shown in Figure 5.1.

Figure 5.1. Example of Self-Efficacy Questions for Planning Topics in C600

Rate your degree of confidence in your ability to perform each of the following tasks by recording a number from 0 to 100 using the scale given below:

Cannot do at all					Moderately can do					Highly certain can do
0	10	20	30	40	50	60	70	80	90	100

Use JOPP to analyze operational-level missions   _____

Use JOPP to analyze and war game the developed
courses of action   _____

Use JOPP to recommend a course of action   _____

Self-efficacy strength is calculated by taking the average ratings across items about a particular construct. The magnitude of self-efficacy can be measured by dividing the number of non-zero responses by the total number of response. For example, if a respondent rated these three items 0,

40, and 50, self-efficacy strength would be 30, i.e., $(0 + 40 + 50)/3$, and self-efficacy magnitude would be 2/3 or 0.67.

However, measures of self-efficacy, when administered only at the end of a course, may reflect pre-existing knowledge rather than knowledge gain. **To assess the impact of the course on learning, a stronger approach is to administer self-efficacy questions before and after training in combination with individual-level explanatory variables** (cognitive ability, e.g., scores on the Nelson-Denny reading test or on another assessment such as the Wonderlic Cognitive Ability test, demographics, learning goal orientation, motivation to learn) measured at the beginning of the course (see Appendix F for measures of learning goal orientation and motivation to learn).[55,56] In order to link pre-training and post-training responses (e.g., answers regarding self-efficacy, and demographic data), this approach would require data on cognitive learning topics to be collected on an identified basis. In other words, we are suggesting that the self-efficacy survey be administered separately from the course/instructor satisfaction survey (discussed below). Results from the demographic and self-efficacy survey could serve as a reasonable proxy for pre-post administration of objective measures of cognitive learning (i.e., knowledge tests), which are time-consuming to develop and administer, particularly for topics involving critical thinking skills.

Second, administer a separate, anonymous post-course survey to assess satisfaction with training. Separating course satisfaction questions to be collected on an unidentified basis from self-efficacy questions will encourage candid responses from students. The satisfaction survey would focus on reactions to training (e.g., questions about satisfaction with assessments and instructional delivery) along with a limited number of explanatory items including component, rank, highest degree, age, career field, payment status (i.e., personal or duty time) while taking the course (for ADL and Phase II TASS students), and questions about time available to work on the course (ADL and Phase II TASS). Individual-level variables would need to be included in each survey, as participation is anonymous and responses across surveys cannot be linked. In addition, note that using standard response options for demographic characteristics (e.g., for degree, use Bachelor's, Master's, Doctorate (PhD, DO, JD), and other) on surveys rather than fill-in-the-blank answers will facilitate analysis.

Third, for questions about cognitive learning - whether concerning self-efficacy or perceived knowledge gain – administer a subset of the detailed questions about each topic or ask more global questions. Typically, asking multiple questions for each construct is recommended to ensure reliability. However, as noted earlier in this report, we suspect that students are unlikely to recall how well they learned the material at the level of detail presented

---

[55] In the resident course, one pre-training survey should be administered at the start of training rather than conducting a survey prior to each block.

[56] This approach uses a quasi-experimental design. A true experiment requires random assignment and a control group. This sort of evaluation is appropriate for research, but it is not conducted routinely for courses in higher education.

in the surveys, particularly for Phase II in TASS and all phases in ADL, which occur over a period of months, and in the last three weeks of the resident course, when four different blocks come to an end. Therefore, continuing to ask many specific questions is likely to produce data with limited variability and to lead to other negative consequences, such as low response rates and missing data. Given that students appear to be generally satisfied with the Common Core, it also may not be necessary to ask extremely detailed questions unless feedback is needed regarding a change to the course. Asking global rather than specific questions was implemented for several topics in Phase II. For example, in ADL and TASS, students answered one general question about battle command: "C400 improved my ability to conduct Battle Command." In contrast, resident students answered four questions (framing the commander's tactical problem, formulating a commander's intent, preparing commander's guidance, and prescribing commander's critical information requirements). Coefficient alpha was 0.94, indicating that students' answers were highly consistent to all four questions, which in turn suggests that fewer questions would have produced the same result. Straus et al. (2011) and The Army Distributed Learning (DL) Guide (TRADOC, 2013) provide sample questions geared toward DL courses. Since this study was completed, CGSS has, in fact, reduced the length of the surveys.

Response burden can be reduced further by sampling students to complete each survey in the resident course or by administering a subset of the items in each phase in ADL and TASS (as CGSS did in Phases II and III). Response rates might be higher if students are aware that they will be asked to complete fewer or shorter surveys. Indeed, CGSS has implemented sampling in their survey practices for the resident course following completion of this study, and they report higher response rates compared to the previous year. At the same time, students should not be prevented from providing feedback; thus, all students can be given the option to complete each survey if they so desire.

Fourth, for objective questions, we recommend moving from five to six response options, e.g., "strongly disagree," "disagree," "disagree somewhat," "agree somewhat," "agree," and "strongly agree." More options are preferable for Likert-type scales because validity and reliability improve as the number of response options increases, up to seven (Lozano, García-Cueto, and Muñiz, 2008), and an even number of options eliminates the middle, ambiguous response of "neutral." A six-point scale is likely to result in more variation in responses, which can enhance the diagnostic value of the survey. In a recent study of another CGSOC course, we found less leniency bias and more variation using a six-point scale (Straus et al., 2013). Greater variation in responses among resident students is especially important to differentiate reactions and attitudes toward the individual blocks, which are each taught by different faculty members. The effect of using these alternative response options for the Common Core could be examined in a pilot with a subset of students.

Fifth, analyze responses to open-ended questions to gain a more thorough understanding of students' experiences in the course and to identify issues not addressed in objective questions. Although analysis of qualitative data can be time consuming, there are a variety of commercial tools that provide automated ways to analyze these types of responses. For example, text-mining software can be used to identify major themes without reading responses word for word, to distinguish between positive and negative comments, and to apply established or customized categories to classify comments.

Sixth, add questions to both surveys to address topics that emerge from responses to the open-ended questions or to diagnose patterns of responses to objective questions (such as higher perceived difficulty in Phase II for ADL students). TASS students in Phase II, many of whom have full-time jobs, frequently commented on the excessive workload and the negative effects on achieving course goals and meeting work and family commitments. Findings from other research suggest that it may be useful to include objective questions about topics such as students' family and job commitments and time available to work on the Common Core and to examine correlations of these responses with perceived cognitive learning. Martinez-Caro (2011) found that student work status was negatively associated with perceived performance in e-learning classes. In addition, studies of working students have found that the need to fulfill roles of both employee and student creates stress that negatively affects well-being and is detrimental to educational goals (Buda and Lenaghan, 2005; Lenaghan and Sengupta, 2007). Martinez-Caro (2011) argues that this role conflict is particularly problematic for e-learning, where the student has primary responsibility for the learning process.

Finally, use web analytics to assess how long students spend on the survey to get a sense of whether they appear to be devoting sufficient time to participating or whether they seem to be "clicking through" the items. The transition of the learning management system to a dotcom will enable CGSS to analyze time spent on the surveys. We discuss uses of web analytics for other aspects of course evaluation below.

Other Methods and Metrics for Evaluating the Common Core

Collect follow-up information and evaluations from graduates and other stakeholders. CGSS relies heavily on surveys of current students. Conducting surveys of Common Core graduates some time after completing the course (e.g., after 6 or 12 months) can be used to seek their assessment of how the course has affected their jobs. CGSC has conducted surveys of graduates in the past, and we recommend doing so on a more regular basis and undertaking systematic analysis of results. Likewise, surveys of supervisors can be used to evaluate whether they have seen any difference in graduates' knowledge or performance. Although the Center for Army Lessons Learned conducts surveys of CGSOC course graduates (e.g., Hatfield et al., 2011), examining the association of performance in training with graduates' subsequent judgments or supervisors' ratings could provide a way to assess the impact of training on job performance. CGSS also administers faculty surveys and conducts focus groups of instructors, students, and brigade commanders. Focus groups, in particular, can be useful to diagnose issues that emerge from survey responses, such as reasons for perceived difficulty of the course or for unclear expectations for ADL students.

In addition to obtaining input from these stakeholders, web analytics can be used to assess different aspects of the Common Core and provide for more comprehensive evaluation of the course. Data collected in many learning management systems can be used to assess student behavior and its association with performance. For example, Sitzmann has found that effort, or time on task, was positively associated with learning in online training (e.g., Sitzmann and Johnson, 2010; 2012). Damianov et al. (2009) examined the association of time spent on the course and GPA obtained from academic records with grades in online business school courses. Time spent on the course was available in their learning management system (Blackboard); these measures were reasonable approximations of effort because Blackboard would log students off after 20 minutes of inactivity. Damianov et al. (2009) found that extra effort helped students move from low grades (F, D, or C) to a B grade, but improvement from a B to an A was dependent largely on GPA. They propose that other measures, such as the number of times a student logs in to the course or number of messages posted on course discussion boards, could also be used to characterize how students learn and how these activities contribute to performance in the course.[57]

More sophisticated use of analytics can also support the learning process directly. Eric Mazur, a Physics professor at Harvard, has a developed a system called Learning Catalytics for this purpose (Parry, 2011; see also Learning Catalytics, not dated). Rather than spending class time in lectures, students prepare for class in advance, e.g., by watching a videotaped lecture online. During class, the instructor poses questions for students to answer using their laptops or mobile devices. Students also input their seat position in the room. Students with different responses are then grouped (either by the system or by the instructor); and the system sends a message to students instructing them to discuss their answers (e.g., "Discuss your answer with Pat Smith who is sitting to your right.") After the discussion, students respond to the question again. In contrast to using clickers to vote on a response, students can submit answers in a variety of formats (e.g., text, graphical). The system not only enables the instructor to monitor students' understanding of concepts in real time, but facilitates collaborative learning. This method has been used primarily for face-to-face classes, but it could also be used to match students working in a DL environment and direct them to an online chat site to discuss their responses (B. Lukoff, personal communication, January 19, 2012).

CGSS could also track student completion rates and time to completion of phases, particularly in ADL, where students are responsible for their progress through the course. This information could be used both to monitor problems in completing the coursework based on particular blocks or phases or on various student characteristics. Completion rates can also be used to assess the efficiency of training (Shanley et al., 2012). While CGSS currently tracks some of these measures, the reliability of these data is uncertain; for example, better accounting

---

[57] We originally intended to analyze web analytics associated with student behavior in ADL lessons in the present study, but the version of Blackboard in use did not have the capability to collect these data.

of students who switch venues during the course is needed to accurately monitor completion rates. In addition, it may be worthwhile to send a brief survey to students who are progressing slowly or who drop out of the course to determine the reasons for these outcomes. In previous work, we found that a large percentage of non-graduates from The Army Distributed Learning Program (TADLP) courses cited reasons associated with the DL courses or policies, including technical problems, lack of support for administrative, course content, or technical issues; issues related directly to the course itself, such as course length or content; and insufficient time available for students who worked on required courses on personal time (Straus et al., 2011).

Organizational Supports Needed for Evaluation Efforts in CGSS

The reliability of data for monitoring, as well as some of the difficulties we have reported in obtaining data (e.g., measures of cognitive ability, component) or obtaining consistent or reliable data (e.g., in surveys), indicate the need for better infrastructure for evaluation within CGSS. Specifically, evaluation could be facilitated through

- availability of systems that integrate needed data including demographic characteristics, measures of cognitive ability, and grades
- use of standardized measures of individual and training characteristics
- sufficient staff with knowledge and skills in survey development and analysis to implement the proposed recommendations.

Concluding Thoughts

Evaluation is an important process in training and education to support improvements in course design and delivery. This study demonstrates many of the challenges in evaluating educational outcomes, particularly for courses that focus on complex cognitive skills. It also demonstrates the difficulties of comparing instructional venues in a field setting in which delivery methods and other factors are inextricably bound. Where these inherent confounds exist, they underscore the importance of focusing on whether the best possible outcomes within venues, rather than equivalent outcomes across venues, are achieved.

APPENDIX A. CGSOC COMMON CORE TERMINAL LEARNING OBJECTIVES

There are 19 primary or TLOs taught or introduced in the Common Core. These are summarized below.[58] The term in parentheses at the end of each summary indicates the cognitive domain level of learning for each TLO based on Bloom's (1956; 1994) taxonomy.[59]

TLO: 701-ILE-1001. Lead in the development of organizations and leaders that achieve results. This objective includes understanding the role of field grade officers as organizational-level leaders and how leaders develop organizations, establish an ethical climate within organizations, manage organizational stress, negotiate and mediate to extend influence. Each student develops an organizational-level philosophy on leadership. (Synthesis)

TLO: 701-ILE-1002 Refine critical thinking skills to solve problems and make decisions. This objective includes examining critical thinking and creative thinking tools, analyzing mental models and developing probable solutions for an ambiguous problem. (Analysis)

TLO 701-ILE-1003 Use historical context to inform professional military judgment. This objective includes analyzing the development of modern warfare using the concepts of major theorists, current doctrine and history, explaining contemporary events using historical analogies, and constructing and defending an argument using historical evidence. (Analysis)

TLO 701-ILE-1004 Analyze the causes, consequences, and contexts of revolutionary changes in modern warfare. This objective includes analyzing military revolutions, the nature of societal, economic, and political revolutions, the historical role of new technology, and the "Western way of war"; and evaluating the impact of World War I. (Analysis)

TLO 701-ILE-1005 Analyze the likely impact of threats, challenges, and opportunities in the international security environment through the next 10 to 15 years. This objective involves considering the contemporary operational environment from both common and conflicting perspectives. (Analysis)

---

[58] The full description of the TLOs is found in Headquarters, U.S. Army Command and General Staff College, 2009.

[59] CGSS uses a version of Bloom's (1956; 1994) cognitive levels. These include

- Knowledge: Recall of specific information
- Comprehension: understanding the material
- Application: Use of knowledge to solve problems
- Analysis: Breaking material down into component parts to determine structures and relationships
- Synthesis: Integrating parts into a new whole
- Evaluation: Judging or weighing by building and using criteria and standards.

TLO: 701-ILE-1006 Develop cultural considerations for military plans and operations. This objective includes being able to explain the importance of culture and cultural awareness in military plans and operations, specifying cultural characteristics relevant to military operations and incorporating cultural considerations into military plans and operations. (Synthesis)

TLO: 701-ILE-1007 Explain joint force and interagency capabilities and limitations, and multinational and legal considerations. This includes being able to explain the roles, functions, capabilities, and limitations of the U.S. Navy, U.S. Coast Guard, U.S. Marine Corps (USMC), U.S. Army, U.S. Special Operations Forces (SOF); U.S. interagency capabilities; multinational considerations; operational legal issues; the fundamentals of strategic communication; strategic national sustainment means; and strategic national logistics strategies/tasks in contemporary operations. (Comprehension)

TLO: 701-ILE-1008 Interpret joint operational doctrine. This objective includes being able to explain the fundamentals of joint operations, joint operation planning, operational art, operational design and assessment, the Joint Operation Planning and Execution System (JOPES), and the range and types of military operations. (Comprehension)

TLO: 701-ILE-1009 Analyze US Army doctrinal concepts. This objective includes examining the concept of battle command, the Army's operational concept of full spectrum operations, and modular force logistic concepts and being able to explain key concepts of the Army's training doctrine and the commander's Design Concept responsibilities. (Analysis)

TLO: 701-ILE-1010 Interpret the Joint Operation Planning Process. This objective includes analyzing an operational level mission, developing operational level courses of action, analyzing and war gaming developed courses of action, assessing war gamed courses of action, and recommending a course of action to gain approval of the joint force commander. (Evaluation)

TLO: 701-ILE-1011 Conduct the military decision making process. This objective includes conducting mission analysis; developing a course of action; and analyzing a course of action. (Synthesis)

TLO: 701-ILE-1012 Employ the joint functions These include command and control, intelligence, fires, movement and maneuver, protection, sustainment, and information operations. (Application)

TLO: 701-ILE-1013 Explain the leader development process. This objective includes analyzing leader development doctrine, describing the leader self-development process, developing self-awareness, and building an Individual Development Plan (IDP) (Synthesis)

TLO 701-ILE-1014 Analyze Department of Defense (DoD) and Army change management processes. This objective includes describing key strategic documents/elements that guide defense/Army transformation, the benefits, limitations, and planning considerations of contract support of military operations, joint and Army capabilities development, force development, the Planning, Programming, Budgeting and Execution (PPBE) system, and the Total Army Analysis (TAA) process; analyzing the impacts of implementing the Future Combat

System as part of Army transformation, the Army Forces Generation (ARFORGEN) concept for effecting relevant and ready forces for operational requirements; and identifying contemporary issues in Force Management. (Analysis)

TLO: 701-ILE-1015 Explain how desired and undesired effects connect military strategic and operational objectives and tactical tasks within the operational environment. This objective includes discussing basic strategic concepts, analyzing the strategic and operational courses of action, the United States national security organization, the defense national military and the national security strategies; describing the organization of the Department of Defense, the Joint Strategic Planning System (JSPS), and Security Cooperation; and formulating a Regional Strategic Concept. (Evaluation)

TLO 701-ILE-1016 Explain the importance of modern media and telecommunications on military operations. This object includes developing a plan for and executing a live media interview and discussing the impact of modern media and telecommunications on military operations. (Synthesis)

TLO 701-ILE-1017 Examine the role of the Professional Military Officer in society. This includes consideration of the theoretical basis of the American civil-military relationship and recent American civil-military relationship experience. (Analysis)

TLO: 701-ILE-1018 Develop a written argument. This objective includes defining a problem, issue, or topic, determining the thesis or controlling idea and the major supporting points, collecting the basic evidence supporting the major points, interpreting the supporting evidence, determining the key ideas for the analysis, writing the key ideas and a persuasive conclusion. (Evaluation)

TLO: 701-ILE-1019 Communicate effectively. This objective includes writing and speaking effectively, and engaging in strategic communications. (Synthesis)

APPENDIX B. EXAMPLES OF SURVEY QUESTIONS AND COEFFICIENT ALPHA STATISTICS FOR SCALES MEASURING PERCEIVED LEARNING AND QUALITY OF ASSESSMENTS

Block	Scale (abbreviation, if applicable)	# items	Examples of Items	Coefficient Alpha
Foundations (C100)	Foundations	6	C100 improved my ability to solve problems through critical thinking C100 improved my knowledge of the Army Leader Development Process	0.88
	Civil-Military Relations[a]	5	C100 improved my understanding of the role of civil-military relations in the current operating environment	0.92
	Individual Development Plan (Ind. Dev. Plan)	1	Preparing the IDP will help me plan my professional self-development	--
Strategic Environment (C200)	Strategic Environment Objectives (Strat. Env. Obj.)	9	C200 improved my ability to explain basic strategic concepts C200 improved my understanding of strategic-level logistics doctrine	0.93
	Strategic Environment Assessments (Strat. Env. Assessmnts)	3	The C200 examination accurately tested my analysis of U.S. defense strategy	0.84
JIIM Capabilities (C300)	Contemporary Operations (Contemp Ops)	4	I can explain Joint Force Capabilities in contemporary operations	0.90
	Multinational Command Relationships Paper (Multinat. Cmd. Paper)	2	The Multinational Command Relationships Paper was a good assignment for me to explain my understanding of multinational command and control structures in contemporary operations	0.93
	JIIM Lessons	11	C300 (JIIM capabilities) lessons improved my ability to: explain the fundamentals of U.S. Space operations explain U.S. Navy capabilities and limitations at the operational level	0.93

Block	Scale (abbreviation, if applicable)	# items	Examples of Items	Coefficient Alpha
Doctrine (C400)	Fundamental of Joint Operations (Joint Ops)[a]	4	I can explain the fundamentals of joint operations as related to joint force organization	0.92
	Joint Operational Design[a]	8	I can explain the following, as related to joint operational design: center of gravity decisive point	0.96
	Battle Command[a]	4	I can conduct battle command by framing the commander's tactical problem	0.94
	Modular Force Logistics (Mod. Force Logistics)[a]	4	I can explain the concept of modular force logistics by explaining logistical operations	0.93
	Commander's Intent (Cmds Intent)[a]	3	Formulating the Commander's Intent improved my ability to articulate key tasks	0.94
	Full Spectrum Operations[a]	4	C400 increased my understanding of how to apply the following elements of Full Spectrum Operations: The offense The defense	0.96
	Guadpres[a,b]	6	The Guadalcanal Presentation was an accurate test of my ability to: Analyze strategic ends, ways, and means Analyze operational centers of gravity	0.98
Joint Functions (C500)	Joint Function of Intelligence (Joint Func Intell)	2	I can apply the joint function of intelligence by describing the role of intelligence at the operational level	0.91
	Joint Function of Fires (Joint Func Fires)	2	I can apply the joint function of fires by describing the joint targeting process	0.93
	Joint Function of Movement and Maneuver (Joint Func Move Mnvr)[a]	2	I can apply the joint function of movement and maneuver by describing operational maneuver	0.85
	Joint Function of Protection	4	I can apply the joint function of protection by describing ways of conserving the joint force's fighting potential	0.91
	Joint Function of Sustainment	5	I can apply the joint function of sustainment by describing the authority for the operational sustainment of a joint force	0.96
	Information Operations	5	I can describe the information operations core capabilities of: Psychological operations Military deception	0.95

84

Block	Scale (abbreviation, if applicable)	# items	Examples of Items	Coefficient Alpha
Planning (C600)	JOPP Analysis	11	As a result of what I learned about using JOPP to analyzing operational-level missions, I can Comprehend the strategic situation As a result of what I learned about using JOPP to analyze and war game the developed courses of actions, I can develop a synchronization matrix As a results of what I learned about using JOPP to recommend courses of action, I can develop a course of action decision brief for the commander	0.96
	JOPP Exam[c]	4	The Operational Planning Exam was a good instrument to test my understanding of joint operation planning terms	0.97
	MDMP	1	As a result of what I learned during the MDMP application I'm confident I can lead a staff in conducting MDMP	--
	GAAT Scenario	7	The Commander's Planning Guidance individual homework (GAAT [Georgia-Armenia-Azerbaijan-Turkey] scenario) was a valid means to assess my ability to understand a tactical item	0.95
History (H100)	History Objectives (History Obj.)	2	H100 improved my ability to use historical context to inform professional military judgment	0.88
	Argumentative Essay (History Arg. Essay)	5	The argumentative essay was a valid assignment for me to analyze the causes of revolutionary change in modern warfare.	0.91
Leadership (L100)	Leadership Objectives (Leadership Obj.)	10	L100 improved my ability to explain how field grade officers lead in the development of organizations and leaders to achieve results Leading Organizations in Change, and the associated case study of the Police Commissioner William Bratton, improved my understanding of how leaders implement change within organizations	0.93
	Leadership Exam (Leader. Exam)	1	The L100 take home exam of the 56th Heavy Brigade Combat Team provided a fair assessment of the organizational topics covered in the L100 Leadership block	--
	Leadership Paper	1	Writing a leadership philosophy in L100 helped me improve my self-awareness as an organizational-level leader	--
Force Management (F100)	Force Management Objectives (Force Mgt. Obj.)[d]	5	I can describe: The key strategy organizations that guide Defense/Army change Army force development	0.90

Block	Scale (abbreviation, if applicable)	# items	Examples of Items	Coefficient Alpha
	Force Management Assignments (Force Mgt. Assignmts.)[d]	2	The Argumentative Essay allowed me to demonstrate my understanding and analysis of the concepts, processes, agencies, and issues of Army Change Management	0.77
	Force Management Analysis	2	I can analyze the impacts of implementing a major Army modernization program	0.80
	Change Management Processes	4	As a result of the instruction I received in F100, I better understand why Army change management is relevant to me as a field grade officer	0.90
	Contract Support of Military Operations	3	Regarding contract support of military operations, I can describe the benefits of contract support of military operations	0.93

NOTE: Italics indicate items or scales measuring perceived quality of assessments. Regular font indicates items or scales measuring perceived learning.
[a]The surveys had multiple item scales in resident and single, general items in ADL and TASS.
[b]Resident and TASS only.
[c]ADL and TASS only.
[d]Used a subset of items in resident that are directly comparable to items in TASS and ADL.

APPENDIX C. SURVEY QUESTIONS AND COEFFICIENT ALPHA STATISTICS FOR SCALES MEASURING INSTRUCTIONAL DELIVERY AND OVERALL SATISFACTION

Phase	Venue	# Items	Coefficient Alpha	Items
			Instructional Delivery	
I	Resident C100	8	0.93	I experienced a collaborative adult learning environment
	Resident C200	8	0.93	The feedback I received enhanced my learning
	TASS	8	---	My experience was valued as part of the group learning
				My faculty members were knowledgeable in the subject matter they taught
				Technology was appropriately integrated into the classroom
				My faculty members encouraged critical reasoning
				My faculty members arrived prepared for class
				The classroom discussions included appropriate examples that supported my learning
	ADL	8	0.79	The ADL lessons encouraged critical thinking
				The ADL lessons included appropriate examples that supported my learning
				The check-on-learning questions helped me learn the course material
				The check-on-learning questions helped me prepare to take the online tests
				Technology was appropriately integrated into the coursework
				The feedback I received enhanced my learning
II	Resident C300	8	0.93	
	Resident C400	8	0.94	
	H100	8	0.92	
	L100	8	0.92	
	F100	8	0.95	
	TASS	8	0.89	

Phase	Venue	# Items	Coefficient Alpha	Items
	ADL	6	0.82	
III	Resident C500	8	0.95	
	Resident C600	8	0.94	
	TASS	8	0.90	
	ADL	6	0.85	
Overall Satisfaction				
I	ADL only	2	0.72	Overall, I was satisfied with the Phase III course
II	TASS and ADL	2	0.80	I would recommend to others that they complete Phase III through [ADL/TASS] instruction
III	TASS	2	0.60	

APPENDIX D. SURVEY RESPONSES IN RESIDENT, ADL, AND TASS VENUES

Figure D.1. Perceived Cognitive Learning in Phase I Across Venues

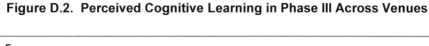

†*p* < 0.10

Figure D.2. Perceived Cognitive Learning in Phase III Across Venues

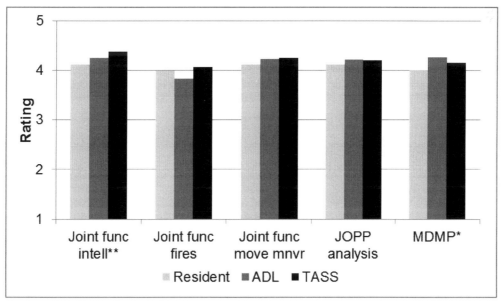

*p < 0.05, **p < 0.01

Figure D.3. Perceived Cognitive Learning in Cross-Cutting (Parallel) Blocks Across Venues

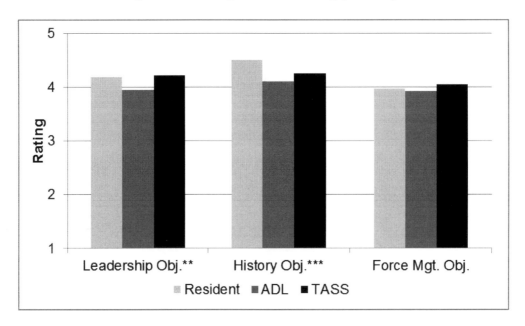

$**p < 0.01, ***p < 0.001$

APPENDIX E. ASSOCIATION OF STUDENT DEMOGRAPHIC CHARACTERISTICS AND SURVEY RESPONSES

Table E.1 below shows the distributions of demographic characteristics among survey participants across ADL and TASS venues. We examined the association of these factors with students' survey responses. In the ADL Phase I survey, component, career field, and payment status variables each showed only one or no significant associations with the other survey measures. The number of significant effects was smaller than one would expect by chance. Reasons for taking the course online showed statistically significant associations with ratings of some aspects of the course; moreover, contrasts comparing students who reported that they prefer learning in an online environment (either as the sole reason for taking ADL or in combination with other reasons) and all other groups show statistically significant results for several measures including three of the learning objectives scales, several assignments, perceived fairness of tests, instructional delivery, and overall satisfaction with the course. Results for a number of other scales or items were marginally significant.

In the ADL Phase II survey, there were no associations of component or career field with ratings of the course. There was only one significant effect of payment status. Given the large number of tests, this result could have occurred by chance. There were no significant associations of component or career field with survey ratings in the Phase III surveys in ADL or TASS. These findings could be interpreted to mean that student characteristics are not associated with reactions to or attitudes toward the course; alternatively, the lack of association could be due to limited variation in responses to most of the survey questions.

Table E.1. Demographic Characteristics of Survey Participants (where available)

Venue	ADL			TASS
Phase	I	II	III	III
Component				
Regular Army	30%	15.5%	20%	1%
ARNG	34%	44%	41%	54%
Army Reserves	30%	40%	39%	45%
Other service	5%	0	0	0
International Military	<1%	0	0	0
Army Civilian	<1%	< 1%	0	0
Career Field				
Maneuver, Fires, and Effects	29%	28%	29%	29%
Operations Support	18%	23%	25%	27%
Force Sustainment	10%	13%	14%	21%
Health Services	29%	21%	20%	17%
Other	9%	14.5%	8%	0
Not applicable or not available	5%	< 1%	4%	6%
Payment Status				
Duty time	18%	14%		
Personal time	69%	65%		
Equal amounts of duty and personal time	13%	21%		
Reasons for taking online course				
Job or other commitments	34%			
No other option	30%			
More convenient	12%			
Prefer online learning	4%			
More than one of the above	20%			

92

APPENDIX F. GRADER CHARACTERISTICS

Table F.1. Grader Characteristics

Variable	Response Options				
Time spent on task	30 min. or less	31-60 min.	61-90 min.	91-120 min.	> 120 min.
	0	10%	26%	29%	36%
Subject matter expertise	Generalist	Specialist			
	35%	65%			
Years grading for CGSOC	< 1	1-2	3-5	> 5	
	8%	15%	35%	42%	
CGSOC courses taken[a]	Common Core	AOC	CGSC Legacy Course		
	87%	89%	82%		
Current or prior experience as CGSOC instructor	Yes				
	82%				
Years of other teaching experience	None	1-2	3-5	6-10	More than 10
	34%	11%	23%	15%	17%
Current status	AC	USAR— M-Day	DoD Civilian	Other Civilian	
	11%	13%	28%	49%	
Years of military experience	20 or more				
	94%				
Highest level of education	Bachelors	Masters	Ph.D.	Other	
	0	77%	21%	2%	
Professional development completed[a]	FDP1	FDP2	FDP3	Other DoD	Other civilian
	83%	88%	60%	17%	10%
Grading guidelines or resources typically used	Rubrics	FD Materials	SOPs	Other	None
	87%	66%	21%	40%	2%

[a] Respondents could select "all that apply" to these questions; therefore, the sum of responses exceeds 100 percent.

APPENDIX G. MEASURES OF LEARNING GOAL ORIENTATION AND MOTIVATION TO LEARN

Learning goal orientations from Button, Mathieu, and Zajac, (1996) (Items 1 – 8 measure performance orientation; items 9 – 16 measure mastery orientation):

1. I prefer to do things that I can do well rather than things that I do poorly.
2. I'm happiest at work when I perform tasks on which I know that I won't make any errors.
3. The things I enjoy the most are the things I do the best.
4. The opinions others have about how well I can do certain things are important to me.
5. I feel smart when I do something without making any mistakes.
6. I like to be fairly confident that I can successfully perform a task before I attempt it.
7. I like to work on tasks that I have done well on in the past.
8. I feel smart when I can do something better than most other people.
9. The opportunity to do challenging work is important to me.
10. When I fail to complete a difficult task, I plan to try harder the next time I work on it.
11. I prefer to work on tasks that force me to learn new things.
12. The opportunity to learn new things is important to me.
13. I do my best when I'm working on a fairly difficult task.
14. I try hard to improve on my past performance.
15. The opportunity to extend the range of my abilities is important to me.
16. When I have difficulty solving a problem, I enjoy trying different approaches to see which one will work.

Selected items measuring motivation to learn, adapted from Noe and Schmitt (1986) and Noe and Wilk (1993):

1. I am willing to exert considerable effort in CGSOC to improve my knowledge and skills.
2. I believe that I can improve my knowledge and skills by participating CGSOC.
3. I will try to learn as much as I can from CGSOC.
4. I will get more from CGSOC than most people will.
5. I would like to improve my knowledge and skills.
6. My present job performance satisfies my personal expectations and goals.
7. Participating in CGSOC is of little use to me because I have all the knowledge and skills I need to successfully perform my job.
8. I am willing to invest effort to improve my knowledge and skills just for the sake of learning.
9. I am willing to invest effort to improve my knowledge and skills in order to prepare myself for a promotion.

References

Alliger, George, Scott I. Tannenbaum, Winston Bennett, Holly Traver, and Allison Shotland, "A Meta-Analysis of Relations Among Training Criteria," *Personnel Psychology*, Vol. 50, 1997, pp. 341–358.

Alvarez, Kaye, Eduardo Salas, and Christina M. Garofano, "An Integrated Model of Training Evaluation and Effectiveness," *Human Resource Development Review*, Vol. 3, No. 4, 2004, pp. 385–416.

Arulampalam, Wiji, Robin Andrew Naylor, and Jeremy P. Smith, "A Hazard Model of the Probability of Medical School Drop-Out in the UK," *Journal of the Royal Statistical Society, Series A: Statistics in Society*, Vol. 167, No. 1, 2004, pp. 157–178. As of January 6, 2012: http://onlinelibrary.wiley.com/doi/10.1046/j.0964-1998.2003.00717.x/pdf

Bandura, Albert, "Guide for Constructing Self-Efficacy Scales," in Frank Pajares and Tim Urdan, eds., *Self-Efficacy Beliefs of Adolescents*, Greenwich, Conn.: Information Age Publishing, Vol. 5, 2006, pp. 307–337.

Bloom, Benjamin S., *Taxonomy of Educational Objectives, Handbook I: The Cognitive Domain*, New York: David McKay Co. Inc., 1956.

———, "Reflections on the Development and Use of the Taxonomy," in Lorin W. Anderson and Lauren A. Sosniak, eds., *Bloom's Taxonomy: A Forty-Year Retrospective*, Chicago National Society for the Study of Education, 1994.

Buda, Richard, and Janet A. Lenaghan, "Engagement in Multiple Roles: An Investigation of the Student-Work Relationship," *Journal of Behavioral and Applied Management*, Vol. 6, 2005, pp. 211–224.

Button Scott B., John E. Mathieu, and Dennis M. Zajac, "The Development and Psychometric Evaluation of Measures of Learning Goal and Performance Goal Orientation." *Organizational Behavior and Human Decision Processes*, Vol. 67, 1996, pp. 26–48.

Cantwell, Robert, Jennifer Archer, and Sid Bourke, "A Comparison of the Academic Experiences and Achievement of University Students Entering by Traditional and Non-Traditional Means," *Assessment and Evaluation in Higher Education*, Vol. 26, No. 3, 2001, pp. 21–34.

Cepeda, Nicholas J., "Distributed Practice in Verbal Recall Tasks: A Review and Quantitative Synthesis," *Psychological Bulletin*, Vol. 132, No. 3, 2006, pp. 354–380.

Clark, Ruth C., and Richard E. Mayer, *e-Learning and the Science of Instruction: Proven Guidelines for Consumers and Designers of Multimedia Learning*, San Francisco, Calif.: Pfeiffer, 2011.

Cohen, Jacob, *Statistical Power Analysis for the Behavioral Sciences,* 2nd ed., Hillsdale, N.J.: Erlbaum, 1988.

Damianov, Damian S., Lori Kupczynski, Pablo Calafiore, Ekaterina P. Damianova, Gökçe Soydemir, and Edgar Gonzalez, "Time Spent Online and Student Performance in Online Business Courses: A Multinomial Logit Analysis," *Journal of Economics and Finance Education,* Vol. 8, No. 2, 2009, pp. 11–22.

Donovan, John J., and David J. Radosevich, "A Meta-Analytic Review of the Distribution of Practice Effect: Now You See It, Now You Don't," *Journal of Applied Psychology*, Vol., 84, No. 5, 1999, pp. 795–805.

Dweck, C. S., "Motivational Processes Affecting Learning," *American Psychologist*, Vol. 41, 1986, pp. 1040–1048.

Fairchild, Ellen E., "Multiple Roles of Adult Learners," *New Directions for Student Services*, No. 102, 2003, pp. 11–16.

Fisher, Sandra L., and J. Kevin Ford, "Differential Effects of Learner Efforts and Goal Orientation on Two Learning Outcomes," *Personnel Psychology*, Vol. 51, 1998, pp. 397–420.

Hatfield, Joshua, John P. Steele, Ryan Riley, Heidi Keller-Glaze, and Jon J. Fallesen, *2010 Center for Army Leadership Annual Survey of Army Leadership (CASAL): Army Education,* Center for Army Leadership, Technical Report 2011-2, April 2011.

Headquarters, U.S. Army Command and General Staff College, *The CGSC Experiential Learning Model,* 2005.

———, *Intermediate Level Education (ILE) Common Core Syllabus*, December 2009.

———, *Information Paper Intermediate Level Education (ILE),* September 23, 2011.

Headquarters, U.S. Department of the Army, *Army Training and Leader Development,* AR350-1, December 2009.

Hoskins, Sherria L., Stephen E. Newstead, and Ian Dennis, "Degree Performance as a Function of Age, Gender, Prior Qualifications and Discipline Studied," *Assessment & Evaluation in Higher Education*, Vol. 22, No. 3, 1997, pp. 317–328.

Kirkpatrick, Donald L., *Evaluating Training Programs: The Four Levels*, San Francisco, Calif.: Berrett-Koehler, 1994.

Klein, Howard J., Raymond A. Noe, and Chongwei Wang, "Motivation to Learn and Course Outcomes: The Impact of Delivery Mode, Learning Goal Orientation, and Perceived Barriers and Enablers," *Personnel Psychology*, Vol. 59, 2006, pp. 665–702.

Koch, James V., "Public Investment in University Distance Learning Programs: Some Performance-Based Evidence," *Atlantic Economic Journal*, Vol. 34, 2006, pp. 23–32.

Kolb, David, *Experiential Learning: Experience as the Source of Learning and Development*, Upper Saddle River, N.J.: Prentice-Hall, 1984.

Kraiger, Kurt, Kevin J. Ford, and Eduardo Salas, "Application of Cognitive, Skill-Based and Affective Theories of Learning Outcomes to New Methods of Training Evaluation," *Journal of Applied Psychology Monograph,* Vol. 2, No. 2, 1993, pp. 311–328.

Learning Catalytics, website, not dated. As of August 11, 2013: https://learningcatalytics.com/

Lenaghan, Janet A., and Kaushik Sengupta, "Role Conflict, Role Balance and Affect: A Model of Well-Being of the Working Student," *Journal of Behavioral and Applied Management*, Vol. 9, No. 1, 2007, pp. 88–100.

Lozano, Luis M., Eduardo García-Cueto, and José Muñiz, "Effect of the Number of Response Categories on the Reliability and Validity of Rating Scales," *Methodology*, Vol. 4, No. 2, 2008, pp. 73–79.

Martinez-Caro, Eva, "Factors Affecting Effectiveness in E-Learning: An Analysis in Production Management Courses," *Computer Applications in Engineering Education,* Vol. 19, No. 3, 2011, pp. 572–581.

Means, Barbara, Yukie Toyama, Robert Murphy, Marianne Bakia, and Karla Jones, *Evaluation of Evidence-Based Practices in Online Learning: A Meta-Analysis and Review of Online Learning Studies,* U.S. Department of Education, Office of Planning, Evaluation, and Policy Development, 2009.

Mesmer-Magnus, Jessica, and Chockalingam Viswesvaran, "Inducing Maximal Versus Typical Learning Through the Provision of a Pretraining Goal Orientation," *Human Performance*, Vol. 30, No. 3, 2007, pp. 205–222.

Miller, Margaret A., and Peter T. Ewell, *Measuring Up on College-Level Learning*, The National Center for Public Policy and Higher Education, October 2005.

Noe, Raymond A., "Trainee Attributes and Attitudes: Neglected Influences on Training Effectiveness," *Academy of Management Review*, Vol. 11, 1986, pp. 736–749.

Noe, Raymond A., and Neal Schmitt, "The Influence of Trainee Attitudes on Training Effectiveness: Test of a Model," *Personnel Psychology*, Vol. 39, 1986, pp. 497–523.

Noe, Raymond A., and Steffanie L. Wilk, "Investigation of Factors that Influence Employees' Participation in Development Activities," *Journal of Applied Psychology*, Vol. 78, 1993, pp. 291–302.

Pajares, Frank, James Hartley, and Giovanni Valiante, "Response Format in Writing Self-Efficacy Assessment: Greater Discrimination Increases Prediction," *Measurement and Evaluation in Counseling and Development*, Vol. 33, 2001, pp. 214–221.

Parry, Marc, "Colleges Mine Data to Tailor Students' Experience," *Chronicle of Higher Education*, December 11, 2011.

Phillips, Jean M., and Stanley M. Gully, "Role of Goal Orientation, Ability, Need for Achievement, and Locus of Control in the Self-Efficacy and Goal Setting Process," *Journal of Applied Psychology*, Vol. 82, 1997, pp. 792–802.

Phipps, Ronald A., and Jamie Merisotis, *What's the Difference? A Review of Contemporary Research on the Effectiveness of Distance Learning in Higher Education,* Washington, D.C.: The Institute for Higher Education Policy, 1999.

Ree, Malcolm James, Thomas R. Carretta, and Mark S. Teachout, "Role of Ability and Prior Job Knowledge in Complex Training Performance," *Journal of Applied Psychology*, Vol. 80, 1995, pp. 721–730.

Ree, Malcolm James, and James A. Earles, "Predicting Training Success: Not Much More Than g," *Personnel Psychology*, Vol. 44, 1991, pp. 321–332.

Shanley, Michael G., James C. Crowley, Matthew W. Lewis, Susan G. Straus, Kristin J. Leuschner, and John Coombs, *Making Improvements to the Army Distributed Learning Program*, Santa Monica, Calif.: RAND Corporation, MG-1016-A, 2012. As of August 7, 2013:
http://www.rand.org/pubs/monographs/MG1016.html

Shrout, Patrick E., and Joseph L. Fleiss, "Intraclass Correlations: Uses in Assessing Rater Reliability," *Psychological Bulletin*, Vol. 86, No. 2, 1979, pp. 420–428.

Sitzmann, Traci, Kenneth G. Brown, Wendy J. Casper, Katherine Ely, and Ryan D. Zimmerman, "A Review and Meta-Analysis of the Nomological Network of Trainee Reactions," *Journal of Applied Psychology*, Vol. 93, 2008, pp. 280–295.

Sitzmann, Traci, Katherine Ely, Bradford S. Bell, and Kristina N. Bauer, "The Effects of Technical Difficulties on Learning and Attrition During Online Training," *Journal of Experimental Psychology: Applied*, Vol. 16, No. 3, 2010a, pp. 281–292.

Sitzmann, Traci, Katherine Ely, Kenneth G. Brown, and Kristina N. Bauer, "Self-Assessment of Knowledge: A Cognitive Learning or Affective Measure?" *Academy of Management Learning & Education*, Vol. 9, No. 2, 2010b, pp. 169–191.

Sitzmann, Traci, Katherine Ely, and Robert Wisher, "Designing Web-Based Training Courses to Maximize Learning," in Kara L. Orvis and Andrea L. R. Lassiter, eds., *Computer-Supported Collaborative Learning: Best Practices and Principles for Instructors*, Hershey, Penn.: Idea Group Inc., 2008, pp. 1–19.

Sitzmann, Traci, and Stefanie K. Johnson, "The Best Laid Plans: Examining the Conditions Under Which a Planning Intervention Improves Learning and Reduces Attrition," *Journal of Applied Psychology*, Vol. 95, 2010, pp. 132–144.

———, "When Is Ignorance Bliss? The Effects of Inaccurate Self-Assessments of Knowledge on Learning and Attrition," *Organizational Behavior and Human Decision Processes*, Vol. 117, 2012, pp. 192–207.

Sitzmann, Traci, Kurt Kraiger, Dennis W. Stewart, and Robert A. Wisher, "The Comparative Effectiveness of Web-Based and Classroom Instruction: A Meta-Analysis," *Personnel Psychology*, Vol. 59, 2006, pp. 623–664.

Straus, Susan G., Jolene Galegher, Michael G. Shanley, and Joy S. Moini, *Improving the Effectiveness of Distributed Learning: A Research and Policy Agenda*, Santa Monica, Calif.: RAND Corporation, OP-156-A, 2006. As of August 7, 2013:
http://www.rand.org/pubs/occasional_papers/OP156.html

Straus, Susan G., Michael G. Shanley, Rachel M. Burns, Anisah Waite, and James C. Crowley, *Improving the Army's Assessment of Interactive Multimedia Instruction Courseware*, Santa Monica, Calif.: RAND Corporation, MG-865-A, 2009. As of August 7, 2013:
http://www.rand.org/pubs/monographs/MG865.html

Straus, Susan G., Michael G. Shanley, Maria C. Lytell, James C. Crowley, Sarah H. Bana, Megan Clifford, and Kristin J. Leuschner, *Enhancing Critical Thinking Skills for Army Leaders Using Blended-Learning Methods*, Santa Monica, Calif.: RAND Corporation, RR-172-A, 2013. As of August 22, 2013:
http://www.rand.org/pubs/research_reports/RR172.html

Straus, Susan G., Michael G. Shanley, Douglas Yeung, Jeff Rothenberg, Elizabeth D. Steiner, and Kristin J. Leuschner, *New Tools and Metrics for Evaluating Army Distributed Learning*, Santa Monica, Calif.: RAND Corporation, MG-1072-A, 2011. As of August 7, 2013:
http://www.rand.org/pubs/monographs/MG1072.html

Talbert-Johnson, Carolyn, "Structural Inequities and the Achievement Gap in Urban Schools," *Education and Urban Society,* Vol. 37, No. 1, 2004, pp. 22–36.

Theroux, James, and Clare Kilbane, "The Real-Time Case Method: The Internet Creates the Potential for New Pedagogy," in John Bourne and Janet C. Moore, eds., *Elements of Quality in Online Education: Engaging Communities*, Needham, Mass.: Sloan-C, 2005, pp. 31–40.

Training and Doctrine Command (TRADOC), *The Army Distributed Learning (DL) Guide*, Fort Eustis, Va.: Headquarters, United States Army Training and Doctrine Command, May 3, 2013.

Wilson, Fiona, "The Construction of Paradox? One Case of Mature Students in Higher Education," *Higher Education Quarterly*, Vol. 51, No. 4, 1997, pp. 347–366.

Wisher, Robert A., Matthew V. Champagne, Jennifer L. Pawluk, Angela Eaton, David M. Thornton, Christina K. Curnow, and Franklin L. Moses, *Training Through Distance Learning: An Assessment of Research Findings,* Final Technical Report 1095, Alexandria, Va.: U.S. Army Research Institute for the Behavioral and Social Sciences, 1999.